Stefan Buczacki

Best Water Gardens

hamlyn

Creative Director Keith Martin
Executive Editor Julian Brown
Designer Tony Truscott
Picture Research Jenny Faithfull,
Liz Fowler, Wendy Gay
Senior Production Controller
Sarah Scanlon

Sections of this book were first published in
Great Britain in 1995 as *Best Water Plants*
This revised edition first published in 2000
by Hamlyn, a division of
Octopus Publishing Group Limited
2–4 Heron Quays, London E14 4JP
© Octopus Publishing Group Limited 1995, 2000
Text © Stefan Buczacki 1995, 2000
Design © Octopus Publishing Group
Limited 1995, 2000

Produced by Toppan
Printed in China

Distributed in the United States by
Sterling Publishing Co., Inc.
387 Park Avenue South, New York,
NY 10016–8810

All rights reserved. No part of this
publication may be reproduced, stored in a
retrieval system, or transmitted, in any form
or by any means, electronic, mechanical,
photocopying or otherwise, without the
prior permission of the publisher

ISBN 0600 60088 2

A catalogue of this book is available at the
British Library

CONTENTS

Introduction 4
How a water garden functions 6
Siting a water garden 8
Formal pools 10
Informal pools 12
Streams and rills 14
Isolated water features 16
Tub gardens 18
Larger, still water pools 20
Fountains, waterfalls and lighting 22
Building a water garden – pre-formed pools 24
Building a water garden – flexible liners 26
Building a water garden – concrete-lined pools 30
Building a water garden – clay-lined pools 32
Water garden maintenance 34
Types of water garden plant 38
Planting, feeding and aftercare 40
Propagation 41
Other pool life 42
Problems 43
Marginals 44
Water plants 60
Submerged plants 74
Floating plants 82
Creating a bog garden 88
Bog garden plants 90
Calendar of water garden jobs 92
Index 94
Acknowledgements 96
Temperature chart 96

INTRODUCTION

I can't think how long it is since I gardened without some form of water feature and, today, I can't imagine going into my garden without hearing the gentle sound of moving water. This book is about gardening with water, the features of which water is an essential part, the way such features can be incorporated into the garden and the range of plants that can be grown in and around the water.

I doubt if water gardening has ever been more popular and yet, paradoxically, as little understood. There is a great deal more to the subject than simply having a garden pool. Modern pumps and low voltage accessories mean that waterfalls, streams and what I call isolated water features (water features without a pond) are now within the reach of every gardener. One enormous, but often overlooked, advantage of the isolated water feature is that it brings the pleasure and sound of moving water into gardens where small children play and where a conventional pool would be inappropriate and dangerous.

In this book I have given information on how to create your own water garden and the pitfalls to be aware of. I describe traditional and modern methods of pool construction as well as the ways in which pools and other water features will fit into your overall garden plan. There is also extensive advice on water garden maintenance and a calendar of water garden care.

A large part of this book covers descriptions of the numerous beautiful water plants that you can use. It is

A wide variety of plants can be grown beside a slow-moving stream

in the area of plant choice that I feel gardeners have been particularly badly served and where garden centres have some catching up to do. Go into the average retail gardening outlet and you will find perhaps three or four water lily varieties, half a dozen other water plants, a dozen marginals and not much more. Little attention is given to plants requiring wet soil – the residents of the bog garden. Retailers cannot be forced to extend their range but I hope that the ever-increasing interest in water gardening and the knowledge that a huge number of desirable plants exists will encourage more gardeners to ask for them.

In several sections of the book I have made reference to pool size in my plant recommendations and while I don't wish this to be interpreted as a rigid rule, I have in mind the following approximate pool sizes in each category: small pools, up to 1.75 x 1.25m (5½ x 4ft) with a maximum depth of about 30cm (12in); medium pools, up to 3 x 1.75m (10 x 5½ft) with a depth of about 45cm (18in); large pools, at least 4.25 x 3m (14 x 10ft) with a maximum depth of at least 60cm (24in).

Water lilies can be combined with pretty marginals in a larger pond

HOW A WATER GARDEN FUNCTIONS

Water gardens are special among garden features in that much of their appeal arises from the various living things that are found there, whether these are naturally occurring or have been introduced by the gardener. Water gardens are also unusual in that the gardener's introductions are not limited to plants because, in order to achieve the necessary balance within the pool, animals are required, too.

Pool water turns green because the mineral salts in the water, the sunlight absorbed by the water and the carbon dioxide given off by plants and fish provide the ideal conditions for single-celled algae to multiply (these minute algae shouldn't be confused with larger, filamentous algae usually called blanket weed). There are times when algae increases to such an extent that they make it impossible to see anything else in the pool. The algae are not, in fact, harmful to fish, which will eat them, but they are unsightly, and controlling them is a matter of achieving the correct balance between all the elements in the pool.

POOL SIZE

Although the siting and the size of a pool and its associated garden are largely a matter of cost and will, ultimately, be determined by the size of your overall garden, it is important to remember that the long-term well-being of the feature and the amount of maintenance required will depend on its size. The smaller the volume of a pool, the more difficult it is to achieve and maintain clear water through establishing a good balance of aquatic organisms. A small volume of water is more likely to be subject to sudden and frequent changes of temperature, and these will stimulate the growth of algae in the water and its subsequent greening. Apart from anything else, of course, a small pool offers little scope for interesting marginal planting, which will also help the good balance of the pool water.

The larger the body of water, the easier it is to maintain a fairly constant temperature, which, in turn, helps to overcome the problems of excess algae by encouraging oxygenating plants. For ease of maintenance, an ideal pool containing still water should have a minimum depth of about 45cm (18in) and a surface area of about 4.5 square metres (50 sq ft). If the surface area is larger than this – more than 9 square metres (100 sq ft), say – all or part of the pool should be 60cm (24in) deep, and a very large pool – or a small lake – should be at least 75cm (30in) deep.

It is worth bearing in mind, however, that there will come a point at which the extra depth serves no additional benefit. It is not, for example, necessary to have a very deep pool for fish to survive all year round. In winter, fish need unpolluted water, and the danger is that, when ice covers the surface for a prolonged period, methane cannot escape. This is the case no matter how deep the pond. It is also often thought that water lilies need very deep water. Although some of the larger varieties do need a large surface area to look their best, most will survive if the crowns are planted at a depth of about 45cm (18in). In much deeper water it will take proportionately longer for the crowns to warm up and start into growth in spring.

PLANTING

Whatever the size of your new pool, it will probably turn green when it is first filled with water, and it may also turn green again each spring. In a well-balanced pool, however, this build-up of algae will be a temporary problem. No pool will be entirely free of algae, but the aim should be to create the conditions in which they are kept to a minimum. In a new pool, the first consideration must be to provide some shade on the water's surface, because algae, as I have indicated above, thrive in sunlight. Water lilies, with their large round pads floating on the water's surface, are the obvious solution, but other floating plants, such as *Hydrocharis morsus-ranae* (frogbit) and *Trapa natans* (water chestnut), will do just as well. Marginal plants also play an important role in providing shade that will help to keep down the temperature of the water and so discourage the proliferation of algae.

The next step is to introduce plants directly into the water to use up the carbon dioxide on which algae thrive. Such plants are known as oxygenators because they release oxygen into the water as a by-product, which is used by fish. The most widely available of these plants is the free-floating *Elodea canadensis* (Canadian pondweed), but *Potamogeton crispus* (curled pondweed) and *Myriophyllum spicatum* (water milfoil), a rooted perennial, are suitable alternatives, especially in small pools. Oxygenating plants tend to grow prolifically – *Elodea canadensis* is notorious in this respect – and will need thinning out regularly every autumn. The aim should be to limit them to no more than one-third of the water volume of the pool.

ANIMAL LIFE

A well-balanced pool will include animal life as well as plants. Snails are useful because they will eat decaying vegetable matter, but they will usually appear in a pond uninvited, introduced on pondweed or brought as eggs on birds' feet.

Fish, which will have to be a conscious introduction, are not only attractive to look at but play an important role in maintaining the balance of gases in the water. They take in oxygen and release carbon dioxide. This carbon dioxide is taken up in turn by the oxygenators and other water plants, and then, through the process of photosynthesis, released as oxygen into the water again.

In addition to eating algae, fish eat aphids and insect larvae, and should also be welcomed to the pool for these reasons.

A water garden is a complex blend of interactions between plants and animals

SITING A WATER GARDEN

The first factor to consider when it comes to siting a pool or water feature is where you will best be able to see it from within the garden itself and, perhaps more importantly, from your house. Because pools are usually built to attract wildlife to the garden or to extend the range of interesting plants you can grow, you will probably want to position your new pool where it is clearly visible, either from a patio or from inside the house – from your kitchen or sitting room, for example. You might also have a favourite sitting area, such as an arbour or summerhouse, within the wider garden.

Part of the attraction of a pool is being able to see reflections in the water's surface – perhaps of clouds being chased across the sky or of nearby statuary or trees and other plants. Make sure that when viewed from your favourite spot, you can enjoy reflections in the surface of the water. This might mean that a long, narrow pool is less appropriate than a wider area, which is more visible from further away. You might even want to find an old mirror or sheet of reflective material and lay it in the garden to give you a better impression of the effect your planned pool will make.

The siting of a water feature in a garden is not simply a matter of selecting a spot in which it will look right and be visible from your favourite sitting place, however, for all pools, both formal and informal, have certain requirements in common.

LIGHT

All pools must have the maximum exposure to sunlight because water plants and most marginals will not thrive in shade, and water lilies in particular, which are so valuable in providing the surface shade that discourages the growth of algae, must have a sunny position if they are to flower. A pool that is sited in the full glare of the midday sun, on the other hand, will need some shade, most easily provided by nearby planting. Spend some time observing your garden and noting the areas that are in sunlight at different times of the day and, if you have time, the year. Remember that the sun is higher in the summer, and that what may be a sunny corner for half the year could be shaded by neighbouring roofs and walls or fences when the sun is low.

Avoid siting a pool directly under or even near to a deciduous tree. Not only will the tree cast unwelcome shade over the water, but the pool itself will suffer when leaves drop into it and decompose in the water, giving off harmful methane gas. The routine scooping out of fallen leaves with a net in autumn will be an essential task no matter where you site your pond, for they are blown considerable distances and seem to be magnetically attracted to open water, but there is no need to make the problem more acute by positioning your pool immediately under a deciduous tree.

Bog gardens, however, may be placed in partial shade, and many of the plants recommended on pp. 90–1 are partially shade tolerant.

WIND

Consider the direction of the prevailing wind in your garden. If the site is very exposed, it may be necessary to erect a wind break in the form of a low fence or hedge. Alternatively, a low bank to a height of about 45cm

An effective combination of water and wood is difficult to achieve

At this stage you should also think about what will happen to the run-off from the pool in periods of very heavy rain. You may not mind the surrounding garden becoming waterlogged from time to time, but the excess water might drain into a neighbour's garden. In these circumstances it would be necessary to build a soakaway to ensure that pond run-off is carried to a much deeper level in your own garden.

Before you make the final decision about the type of pool you want to build, check the house plans or the plans held by your local planning authority to ascertain the position of any pipes or mains conduits. At this stage, too, decide if you will want to introduce a pump or filtration system or lighting of some kind and think about where the electricity cable will run. It is a good idea to dig a trial trench across the area you have chosen. You may find that the subsoil is so rocky that a raised or partially raised pool is a more practical solution than a wholly sunken one.

Even without a pool, individual water features can enhance your garden

(18in) around one side of the pool could be created to provide the necessary protection, using the soil that is removed when you excavate a hole for the pool, or for a dense planting.

SLOPES
Do not site your pool in what may appear to be the most obvious place in the garden – that is, in the lowest part. A pool that stands alone at the foot of a slope will create problems, because it will almost certainly flood in winter. In addition, if you have used a flexible liner, there is a very real danger that in prolonged rainy weather, the water table may rise and cause the liner to rise with it. The lowest point in the garden is also an unwise choice if you are a gardener who uses fertilizer and other chemicals, simply because the run-off into the pool will, at best, make the water turn cloudy and, at worst, poison the wildlife. Level ground at the foot of a slope is ideal, however, if you also plan to have a bog garden, because the moisture in the soil will be constantly replenished by rainwater draining downhill.

SAFETY
Finally, safety must be a consideration in all gardens, especially if children – your own or those of visitors – are likely to be playing outside. Children have been known to drown in just a few centimetres of water. If you are building a water garden from scratch, you may want to consider making a small water feature such as a bubble fountain or wall-mounted spout in which the body of water is contained in a reservoir or sump that is hidden below the ground and whose surface is completely covered.

9

FORMAL POOLS

The formal pool has hard edges of stone, brick or slabs, which create a more or less angular boundary in a paved courtyard or on a terrace, patio or similar area. There is no doubt where the pool ends and the surrounding area begins, and the whole is unashamedly artificial but none the worse for that. The formal pool is often enhanced by some form of fountain or ornamental fountain head or maybe even a sculpture.

The largest, finest and most spectacular water gardens in the world are all quite formal creations. Notable examples include the fountains of the Villa d'Este, Tivoli, near Rome, those at the Palace of Versailles, the Alhambra in Grenada and the cascade at Chatsworth House in Derbyshire in the Midlands of England. The courtyard gardens of the Alhambra, for example, contain large formal pools, linked by canals and embellished and enlivened by fountains, which bring movement and sound into the complex of buildings, which might otherwise have appeared too severe and unwelcoming. The pools were designed and positioned to enhance the Moorish architecture and to add interest by reflecting it back to the viewer. At Chatsworth, where the garden was re-landscaped by Lancelot (Capability) Brown, are the well-known Seahorse Fountain and Great Water Staircase.

Few gardeners today, of course, have either the space or the money to re-create such wonders, but visiting these masterpieces and seeing how water can be used to create effects and heighten atmosphere can be helpful when it comes to planning the features that your own new pool might have.

SHAPE AND STYLE

As I have said, a formal pool is likely to be positioned on a patio, in a courtyard garden or, to use the vogue term, in a 'garden room', a comparatively small, discrete area within the wider garden. The pool will be of a regular geometric shape — a rectangle, a square, or a circle — or a combination of such shapes. It need not be precisely symmetrical — two intersecting square pools on different levels, for example, would be extremely effective — but it will always have straight or smoothly curved sides.

A formal pool must always be in proportion to its surroundings, and the materials used to build it and surround it must be in keeping with those used for the house or walls near it. When it is constructed on a patio a pool with straight, regular edges will be in harmony with the walls of the house and the straight lines of the bricks and paving that butt up to it. The materials used for the patio and pool adjoining a house built of red brick will not be the same as those

Water lilies can be used to break the surface of a formal sunken pool

Formal pools can be grand or simple but all have hard, regular edges

chosen for a pool in a courtyard paved in York stone or one in an enclosed garden where one or more of the walls is of whitewashed rendering. Safety must also be a consideration here. A desire to have as large a pool as possible should not lead to its being surrounded by paths that are too narrow or ones with awkward corners, which will result in difficult and potentially dangerous access for pool maintenance.

RAISED POOLS

Formal pools are often raised. It is, perhaps, easy to imagine such a feature as a raised bed filled with water instead of soil. The basic construction method is similar to that required for a conventional pool, except that a stone or brick retaining wall takes over the function of the hole and it is lined with a flexible liner bedded on sand or some form of pre-formed liner, such as a fibreglass pool or some kind of tank.

Raised pools can look very attractive set in the midst of a formal courtyard planting. Some of the most successful raised pools are circular, and one of the loveliest examples is in the well-known gardens of Hidcote Manor in Gloucestershire, England. Such pools are also greatly appreciated by gardeners who, through age, infirmity or disability, find it difficult to bend down to soil level.

SUNKEN POOLS

Advances in building technology mean that a formal sunken pool can now be made from concrete, formerly an unreliable material which was prone to cracking. Although such a pool involves considerable work, a visit to the gardens of Tintinhull, Somerset, for example, or those of Hidcote, in Gloucestershire, might well provide sufficient inspiration to make you rethink your pool plans. Such sunken pools benefit from rather restrained planting.

The main drawback that a formal pool has for many gardeners is the limited scope for planting marginal plants on ledges just below the surface of the water. The remainder of the planting around the edges of the pool must, through necessity, be of plants in containers, and these, of course, will therefore not be water garden species. The water garden enthusiast who is also a lover of plants will almost certainly want an informal pool around which to grow these marginal plants.

11

INFORMAL POOLS

The informal or semi-natural pool is more versatile than its formal equivalent, for it merges gently at the edges with other planting environments – marginal areas and bog gardens, which themselves vary from the very wet to drier parts, before imperceptibly developing into normal garden beds and borders, shrubberies and even rock gardens. Such an arrangement lends itself perfectly to the inclusion of the widest possible range of plants, which is, of course, what most gardeners want.

The edges of an informal pool are irregular, and any movement of water will be more appropriately provided by gentle waterfalls than by the fountains, so appropriate in the formal pool. In very large gardens, semi-natural pools may even draw their inspiration from natural lakes.

In an informal pool that is well-designed and well-constructed, there should be a smooth transition from the pool proper to the moist or boggy soil around it, because it is in this area, the marginal zone, that the full range of marginal and bog plants can be grown. A formal pool may, of course, have ledges within the limits of the pool, but it is the planting that goes right up to the water's edge and yet at the same time merges with the background planting that is one of the great pleasures of the informal pool. Such areas provide the conditions for a wonderful range of plants, from irises and primulas to grasses and rushes, from large-leaved rodgersias to dainty fritillaries. These areas are perfect for many native species but also provide a micro-climate in which more unusual plants can thrive. In addition, this mass of diverse planting provides an ideal habitat for a wide variety of wildlife.

PRE-FORMED POOLS

Pre-formed pools, with their smoothly curved sides and regular kidney shapes, are often used as the basis of an informal pool, but far too frequently the effect is spoiled by the use of what is all too appropriately known as 'crazy' paving around them. Such an arrangement makes interesting marginal planting impossible, and consequently the pool becomes an isolated feature, neither properly informal nor satisfactorily formal.

It is possible to use a pre-formed pool in an informal setting by sinking it flush into the ground and by disguising the edges with a single course of paving stones, mortared securely in position. The area around the pool can then be planted up. It is important to bear in mind, however, that the surrounding planting will have to be of subjects that will grow in normal garden soil because the water is contained entirely within the pool, and there is no natural marginal area. Nevertheless, carefully planted, such an arrangement has much to recommend it, especially if the pre-formed pool is the largest size for the space available and the ledges within the pool are used for the widest possible selection of water plants.

Most often, however, the informal pool will be created through the use of a flexible liner, although enthusiasts for true wildlife pools may prefer to use clay (see pp.32–3). The aim is to use the liner not only to create a pool with a range of internal levels but also to extend the area around the pool to provide an appropriate environment for plants that thrive in marshy or boggy ground but that do not like to sit in water permanently.

POSITION AND SIZE

The position and size of the informal pool require just as much thought and planning as those of the formal pool. The constraints on siting a pool that I outlined on pp.8–9 are just as relevant here, if not more so, since an informal pool must, above all, appear as if it was always meant to be precisely where and how it is.

Even if you have little artistic skill, draw a scaled plan of your garden and indicate on it the position and dimensions of the proposed pool and of any associated bog garden. Next, draw in the position and, if possible, the spread of nearby trees and established shrubs, and indicate the location of existing hard features, such as paths and fences or retaining walls.

Think, too, about access to all parts of the pool, remembering to consider the different tasks that will need to be carried out at different times of the year. Not only must you be able to tend to the plants in the garden around the edges of the pool, but you need to be able to clear away plant debris from the pool itself with relative ease, and to carry out routine maintenance tasks, to pumps for example. A bog garden that is so wide that you cannot get near choice plants without trampling on others will defeat its object.

An informal pool should blend imperceptibly into the surrounding planting

STREAMS AND RILLS

For many gardeners the ultimate water garden has a stream running throughout it. The sound of running water and the way that it catches the light are among the great delights of the water garden, especially when the sound helps to mask the other noises that intrude from beyond one's own garden boundaries. Unless you are fortunate to have a natural watercourse in your garden, however, introducing such a feature can be an expensive, difficult and time-consuming task. In addition, although modern recirculating pumps have made the creation of the flow of water technically possible, the building of a stream that looks entirely natural is not easy. Unless you are very skilful and are prepared to invest a great deal of time, introducing a stream is not a task to be undertaken lightly.

A small waterfall in a natural stream creates movement in the garden

PLANNING

If you are among the lucky few who have running water in their gardens, make sure that any plans for incorporating the stream into your own water garden comply with local authority regulations before you begin to plant up the banks and certainly before you attempt any construction work that would affect the flow of the water. Although you may own the land over which the stream flows, you will not own the water nor will you have the rights to change anything. Indeed, you may not even be allowed to fish in it.

Even when you are absolutely certain that you will not breach any regulations or bye-laws, remember that few aquatic plants thrive in swiftly running water and that any plants on the stream banks will probably have to survive being immersed for much of the winter and dried out for much of the summer. For such an area you should consider native species that grow naturally in such conditions and concentrate on them.

Given the size of most modern gardens, it is more likely that a gardener who yearns for running water will have to construct an enclosed system, running between two or more separate pools. Modern butyl liners, rigid stream sections and submersible pumps make this a perfectly practicable proposition, even though, as I have suggested already, it requires considerable skill to make the stream appear entirely natural. The first requirement, of course, is a slight gradient – a body of water joining two pools on the same level is less a stream than a long pool. The second requirement is distance – a stream that falls only a short distance between two pools is a waterfall. Angling the pools and stream across your garden may provide the necessary distance, and even if your garden is flat, the spoil removed to create the lower pool can be used to provide additional height for the upper pool. The slope should not be too steep however, for the pump will perform the function of the stream's natural flow. A gradient of about 25cm (10in) over a distance of 3m (10ft) will be sufficient.

While pools, both formal and informal, can function perfectly well without moving water, your preparations for a stream garden must include the position and provision of a low-voltage electrical supply. You must also consider the quantity of water needed to keep both the header (top) and reservoir (bottom) pools full and the stream bed covered when the stream is operating. And, because you will neither want nor be able to run the pump continually all day, every day, consider how you can retain sufficient water in the pools and stream when the pump is switched off.

The course of a natural-looking stream can be constructed comparatively easily if strips of flexible plywood are attached to pegs, which are then driven into the ground to mark the banks of the stream. Butyl liner is laid over the stream bed between the plywood strips and covered with stones and cobbles, which should be mortared in place. Because the plywood is so narrow, planting can take place right up to the water's edge. Alternatively, use a pre-formed stream base. If you prefer to have an associated bog garden, use butyl liner to cover not only the bed of the stream but an area extending beyond it. The course of the stream itself is bounded by stones and cobbles mortared in position over the liner, which should extend beyond the stream and can be covered with soil. Do not forget to pierce holes in the liner used for the bog garden or it will quickly become completely waterlogged. Remember, too, that if you are using more than one piece of butyl liner to line the stream, begin at the lowest point and work upwards.

RILLS

In a formal garden the stream is likely to be replaced by the rill. Visitors to Hestercombe, Somerset, and the Deanery, Berkshire, will have seen just how Edward Lutyens's mastery of the form brought a coherence and emphasis to vistas, directing the viewer's attention to focal points and other features, while providing a beautifully proportional counterpoint to the nearby planting. The gardener working within a more limited area can draw inspiration from Lutyens's work by using paved edges to a narrow rill to emphasize the lines of a garden and to lead the eye and draw attention towards features such as a statue or fountain or a particularly fine tree or shrub.

Modern circulating pumps make small waterfalls relatively easy to create

ISOLATED WATER FEATURES

In a small garden some form of self-contained, re-circulating fountain can be very satisfying, for it combines the appealing trickling sound of moving water with the absence of open water, which can be dangerous if children play in the garden. It is also possible to create a small-scale, modern version of a classical wall fountain, with an ornamental spout from which water cascades into some form of collecting trough before draining away to a concealed tank or sump. Whichever type of feature you choose, make sure that it is in proportion to its surroundings and that its style and the materials you choose are in keeping with the garden as a whole and your house.

BUBBLE FOUNTAINS

The bubble or pebble fountain is one of the most popular of the self-contained water features, providing the maximum sound of tinkling water with the minimum chance of being a danger to children. This type of feature is suitable for a patio or for the wider garden, where it can be made, for example, into the centre of a small natural area, surrounded by ferns and hostas and other moisture- and shade-loving plants.

You will need to excavate a hole sufficiently large to accommodate the water reservoir or sump. If the fountain is to be positioned on a patio, bear this in mind from the start and consider if the work involved in excavating beneath what may be a paved surface is worthwhile. A bubble fountain does not really lend itself to being raised too far off the ground, which would be necessary if you could not accommodate the reservoir below ground level. If this is the case, you might want to consider an alternative feature for such a position.

Because it will not be visible, you can use an old plastic dustbin or any other large watertight container for the reservoir or sump. The fountain works in the following way: a submersible pump stands on bricks in the bottom of the reservoir, and the pipe through which the water is forced upwards is fed through a hole in the centre of a sheet of galvanized mesh. The mesh is laid over the reservoir and is itself covered with a mass of cobbles or a single millstone with a hole through the centre and surrounded by smaller stones. Water is forced up through the feed pipe and cascades over the stones and cobbles, and runs back into the reservoir beneath the mesh. The cable to the mesh can be easily hidden under the stones and gravel.

WALL-MOUNTED FOUNTAINS

Another popular form of self-contained water feature, which again requires a reservoir of some kind, is the wall-mounted fountain. Such features can either have water cascading into a small pool at the foot of a wall or the water can fall down a wall and into a hidden reservoir. Safety considerations might suggest that the latter arrangement is selected, but even a small pool offers opportunities for growing water plants – not water lilies, of course, which do not like continual splashing, but there are many other water and marginal plants that will enjoy such a situation.

There are many different styles of wall-mounted spouts, ranging from the traditional gods' and lions' heads and dolphins to modern, geometric designs in metal. Some models incorporate a small basin beneath the delivery spout, in which the water collects before trickling down into the larger pool or disappearing into the hidden reservoir, and you can even buy chains, down which the water drips before being returned via the pump to the top of the chain again. Fibreglass is now widely used, which means that such features are not only relatively inexpensive but also comparatively light and therefore do not need an exceptionally sturdy wall to support them. Do not, however, be tempted to mount such a feature against an existing house wall, since the continual presence of water may cause damage, no matter how carefully and thoroughly you have prepared the surface.

The water spouts of wall-mounted fountains are as simple to erect as the bubble fountains, but you should bear in mind that you need to have access to both sides of the wall – the pipe delivering the water to the spout will run up one side and be angled through a hole in the wall. The opening of a lion's mouth for example, if that is your choice, should be positioned over the end of the pipe. The water runs through the pipe, emerging as if from the lion's mouth, down the wall and into a reservoir or pool, from where it is pumped up, behind the wall, to fall again.

Wall-mounted fountains can be striking; but you must own both sides of the wall

TUB GARDENS

The tub garden is suitable for those who long for a water feature, but have very small gardens. The wooden half-barrel is most often seen, but any watertight container can be used, and there are some very attractive ceramic containers that are both deep enough and wide enough to be used as water features. Old sinks, which are still occasionally found, have pleasing proportions, especially when they contain some upright-growing flowering plants, such as irises, and rushes, such as *Juncus effusus*.

HALF-BARRELS

If you are using a half-barrel, the first consideration is to make sure it is watertight. A brand-new tub should be waterproof, and probably all you need do is to clean it out thoroughly and then apply a proprietary sealant, to both protect the wood from the water and prevent anything noxious from seeping from the wood into the water. If you are at all unsure about the waterproof qualities of the tub, line it with black heavy-duty polythene or PVC, which can be held in place with galvanized tacks or nails around the top outside edge. Make sure you do not pierce the liner or tub below the proposed water level. Trim away the excess.

SINKS

If you have an old sink that you would like to turn into a mini-pool or, indeed a trough garden for plants, coat the outer sides and the top edges with hypertufa, which can be mixed from 2 parts peat or, preferably, peat substitute, 1 part cement and 1 part coarse sand. Water is added to make a stiff mixture rather like porridge, which can be applied to the sink's surface. Block the drainage hole either with an ordinary plug or with the plastic top of an appropriately sized yoghurt pot, fixed in position with a proprietary waterproof cement.

If you like the idea of the hypertufa trough but do not have an old sink that you can cover, you can make an

Tub gardens give the pleasure of a water garden but on a reduced scale

equivalent by using two wooden formers, one about 5cm (2in) smaller in all directions than the other. The hypertufa can be spread in the base of the larger former before the smaller one is placed inside it. Hypertufa can then be used to fill the gap left between the two formers. Remember to coat the inside of the larger former and the outside of the smaller one with oil so that they can be easily removed when the hypertufa is set, which should take about a week. For extra strength, add some small-mesh wire netting, which can be positioned in the centre of all five (the base and four sides) hypertufa layers.

The problem with small water features, especially those such as tubs and ceramic containers that do not have thick sides, is that they are subject to sharp and sudden fluctuations in temperature, which makes it difficult to keep the water free of algae. Even when the container holds about 25 litres (5 gallons) of water, which is the minimum you should consider practicable, it might overheat in summer or freeze solid in a prolonged period of cold winter weather, even if it is placed near the shelter of a house wall or on a protected patio. Such small containers are not, therefore, suitable for fish or precious plants.

PLANTING

Small water features need to contain oxygenating plants just as much as large pools do. Once these are in place, however, you can add as many or as few other plants as you wish. In a limited space such as a tub, it is always wise to plant each type in a separate container, wrapping the soil and rootball of each in hessian and covering the top of the container with gravel or pebbles to keep the soil in place. This has the advantage that the roots of different plants do not grow into each other and become tangled, and it is then a simple matter to remove any single plant that is failing to thrive or that has become too large for the container and needs to be divided, without having to disturb the other plants in the tub.

Although most water lilies are far too robust and large-growing for a tub, there are a few cultivars that will survive in a limited space. *Nymphaea* 'Pygmaea Helvola' has canary yellow flowers, *N. tetragona* has white flowers, and *N.* 'Pygmaea Rubra' has dark pink flowers. *N.* 'James Brydon' also adapts to the limited confines of a tub and produces fragrant, deep pink flowers in summer, even (unusually for a water lily) when grown in shade.

This is just about the limit – a pond in a bowl

LARGER STILL-WATER POOLS

Few gardens will have room to accommodate a still-water pool with a surface area larger than about 5 square metres (55 sq ft), and many gardeners would, in any case, regard such a large, unplanted area as a waste of space. These days, when there is so much pressure on every inch of the garden to provide play areas for children, a patio for eating and entertaining, borders for cut flowers for the house and vegetable gardens for produce for the kitchen, it would be a brave gardener who is prepared to devote a large area to water. Nevertheless, there is something ineluctably calming about watching the reflections of clouds being chased across the sky in the calm surface of an expanse of water, or being able to see birds swoop across a pool in search of insects.

JAPANESE INFLUENCES

The Japanese garden has much to teach gardeners in the West about the value of stillness, and water is an important factor in what might be called the Zen-style garden. The smooth surface of an expanse of water is an essential part of the Eastern garden, to such an extent that when real water is not present, it is generally represented by raked gravel, with carefully positioned stones standing for waterfalls, bridges, cascades and mountains, and topiarized trees and shrubs standing for clouds and distant hills. When water is included, carefully pruned trees and shrubs are selected to be reflected in its surface.

This small lake is a tranquil spot to relax

LAKES

Enthusiastic gardeners are more likely to admire natural and man-made lakes from afar than to wish to include them within the boundaries of their own gardens, but many of the finest can be visited and can prove to be wonderful sources of inspiration. Among the loveliest examples in Britain is the great lake at Stourhead, Wiltshire. The garden itself covers more than 160 hectares (400 acres) and the walk around the lake is more than 2km (1½ miles) long, but the owner Henry Hoare II and his architect, Henry Flitcroft, created unforgettable vistas with temples, grottoes and statues, and visitors today can hardly fail to be impressed and inspired by the year-round colour provided by the lake-side planting and the unexpected and heart-stopping glimpses of the various focal points that are positioned around the water's edge.

WATER LILIES

If you have space in your garden for a large informal pool you will be able to grow some very fine water lilies. The British native, *Nymphaea alba*, which is also found over a wide part of the continent of Europe and into Asia, is generally found in large lakes or in slow-moving streams and rivers. It is a hardy plant but is far too large for most pools. The lovely cup-shaped, later star-shaped, flowers are up to 20cm (8in) across, with a mass of yellow stamens surrounded by the snowy white petals. The dark green leaf pads, which are up to 30cm (12in) across, are often reddish-green on the reverse. This will grow to 1.8m (6ft) or more across. Another beautiful water lily for a large pool is *N.* 'Gladstoneana', which produces starry white flowers, to 18cm (7in) across, with a mass of golden-yellow stamens. The dark green leaves are to 30cm (12in) across. Lovely though it is, 'Gladstoneana' is suitable only for a very large pool – 1.2m (4ft) would not be too deep – as it will spread to 2.4m (8ft). In smaller pools, both these water lilies can be kept under control by regular lifting and dividing.

FORMAL POOLS

A formal pool will, as we have noted, be surrounded by paving, which defines both the pool and space around it and beyond it. The large formal pool situated at Tintinhull, Gloucestershire, is an inspiring combination of both planting and hard landscaping that might well encourage you to aspire to have in your own garden a similar sunken, formal pool containing just a few carefully positioned irises and water lilies and surrounded by paving on which stand a few thoughtfully planted containers. The essence of this pool is the restrained use of plants that serve to enhance the architecture of the pool and its surroundings.

The delights of a still-water pool lie in the changing pattern of reflections

FOUNTAINS, WATERFALLS AND LIGHTING

Water gardens really come into their own when there is some water movement, such as a waterfall in an informal pool or a fountain in a formal one. If your planning and building work includes electricity for a pump, you should also consider the possibility of providing lighting in your garden.

No matter how much of the work of excavating the pool, laying the liner and creating a firm paved edge you carry out yourself, introducing electricity into the garden, especially when it is used in conjunction with water, is a job for an expert. It cannot be said too often that installing mains voltage wiring into the garden is not a task that should be undertaken by the amateur. Seek professional advice at the planning stage about the routing of cables and ask a qualified electrician to install the system for you.

FOUNTAINS

Anyone who has built a pool as an area for wildlife or as a natural feature will not want to include a fountain. In a formal pool, however, a fountain can be introduced to provide both movement and sound. If you have a formal square or circular pool, a central fountain provides the perfect finishing touch, while a rectangular pool may lend itself rather better to a fountain that arises from a poolside ornament or statue.

There are no hard and fast rules about the type of fountain you should have, and the choice is vast. It ranges from small bubble and millstone fountains through poolside ornaments of many sizes – including figures of humans, animals and birds – to surface jets and statuettes for the centre of the pool. There are water spouts and sprays of various kinds – single, multi-tiered and whirling – in numerous styles, from geysers and fishtails to tulips, bells and rings. Figures and ornaments are also available in a wide range of materials, from traditional lead and stone to modern, lightweight fibreglass and reconstituted stone.

An unusual but striking combination of a fountain with roses

The fountain should take no more than about 50 per cent of the total pool area, and kept in proportion to your pool. In doing so it is not only the size of the ornament that you need to consider. A tall, multi-tiered spray may appear to be just what you want when you see it in the garden centre or in a public park, but before you buy, think what it will look like in your own garden, where it will be seen against the background of your neighbour's fence or against the backdrop of your vegetable garden and compost heap. In even moderately windy weather, a tall plume of water may shower your neighbour's garden (and your neighbours) while scarcely adding at all to the charm of your own garden. Remember, too, that the upward movement of a fountain rarely looks either realistic or attractive when it is combined with the downward movement of a waterfall.

When you are choosing a fountain, do not select one that creates too much water spray because this can have an excessive cooling effect on the pool, to the overall detriment of the fish and plants. When it comes to combining a fountain with your pool plants, remember that water lilies in particular do not thrive if they are continually subjected to a spray of droplets on their leaves, and neither do they tolerate the continual disturbance of fast-moving currents. In such conditions, their leaves often rot or the flowerbuds fail to open or both. If you are particularly keen to grow water lilies in your pool, you will only be able to have a fountain as well if the pool is very large indeed, and you keep the two apart.

Within these constraints, however, many possibilities can be achieved with a modern, low-voltage submersible pump with watertight seals and magnetic couplings. The pump remains permanently immersed and is connected to the mains via low-voltage wire, run from a transformer at the nearest indoor socket to avoid the danger that arises when electricity and water are mixed. Such a pump can be used to great effect by anyone with a basic knowledge of DIY techniques by adapting the outlet to enable it to be attached to, say, an antique lead fountain-head spout.

WATERFALLS

Modern pumps, both submersible and non-submersible, have made it a fairly straightforward matter to introduce a waterfall into a pool, and including such a feature as part of a wildlife or natural pool is an excellent way of aerating the water without the artificiality of a fountain. Unless the pool is very large and the necessary pumping back of water has to be carried out against a considerable gradient, low-voltage DIY pumps will be perfectly adequate.

The waterfall can be made from butyl liner or from concrete, or you can use a pre-formed rigid unit, which will have two or more linked pools. When you are creating your own pools and cascades, bear in mind that the pool areas must have a small lip or must slope backwards slightly so that water is held in the header and reservoir pools even when the pump is not in operation.

LIGHTING

Pool lighting is very much a matter of personal taste. Once again, modern low-voltage systems are inexpensively and easily laid, and the systems that are available range from simple single spotlights used to highlight individual plants or features to more complex coloured submarine lighting.

One aspect of garden lighting that is often overlooked is the need for safety around a pool, especially if your garden is used for entertaining. Low-level lamps along the edge of a path (especially one that includes steps or other changes of level and corners) and around the hard landscaping of a sunken pool, or lamps raised on posts and pillars or along one side of a pergola near a natural pool will serve the dual purpose of enhancing your garden at night and ensuring the safety of both you and your visitors.

Be careful not to allow your waterfall to disappear behind vegetation

BUILDING A WATER GARDEN –

Using pre-formed pool liners, which in many ways resemble large bathtubs for babies, is the cheapest and quickest way of creating a pool, but they do have some drawbacks, the chief of which are that the shape and the positions of the ledges are determined by the manufacturers, leaving you with little scope to use your own imagination, and that the largest size will be about 3.5m (about 12ft long). For convenience, however, a pre-formed pool has much to offer, and they are widely available from garden centres and the larger DIY stores. Skilful marginal planting will soon disguise the outlines and allow the pool to merge with the rest of the garden. Make sure that you choose one that is made from fibreglass and is resistant to ultraviolet light and that has a manufacturer's guarantee of at least 15 years. Look out, too, for a pool that is grey or another neutral colour, so that it will blend with the garden more successfully than the common bright blue.

RAISED POOLS

Pre-formed pools can be used as raised, free-standing features or as partially raised pools or they can, as we have seen, be sunk into a hole so that they are flush with the surrounding garden. A raised pool is one type of water feature that lends itself rather well to the use of a pre-formed liner. A raised pool isn't, as you might think, a pool hovering in mid-air, but in effect is one placed within a raised bed confined by walls. This can make a very striking garden feature in its own right (witness the wonderful example at Hidcote in Gloucestershire) and can also provide an ideal way to bring the pleasure of water gardening to wheelchair gardeners.

If pre-formed units are used as a raised or semi-raised pool, they must be given very strong support because the water pressure in even a comparatively small pool is enormous. Such arrangements are often seen near small rock gardens, where the pool merges at one side into the raised stones, rocks and plants while the other side, disguised by a stone or brick wall or even log rolls abuts the lawn or patio. If your raised pool is bounded by grass, remember to incorporate a mowing strip next to the pool so that you do not have to cut around the sides of the pool by hand – a strimmer will send showers of grass clippings into the pool.

INSTALLING

Build a retaining wall, just as you would for a normal raised bed, of the same shape as the pre-formed pool but with about 30cm (12in) extra all around. I strongly advise that you have the wall built by a professional bricklayer and ensure they are aware of the depth and size of the pool that it will contain so they can guage the necessary size of the wall. The outward pressure of a huge weight of water will be considerable. Once the containing wall is complete, line the whole with sand on which the pre-formed pool can then be placed for a snug fit.

SUNKEN POOLS

If you are using a pre-formed pool as a quasi-natural or sunken pool, iden-

Remember to mark out the perimeters of a pool before starting to dig

PRE-FORMED POOLS

Use a spirit level to ensure the sides of the new water garden are level

tify the best position, lay the pre-formed liner on the ground, supporting it with bricks so that it does not wobble, and mark its position on the ground. You can use pegs, but it is easier to use canes, which can be inserted around the circumference of the pool vertically into the ground. Use a flexible hosepipe or rope to mark the outline of the pool on the ground. At this stage it is worth going back to your patio or kitchen window to check that the position really is the one you want. Of all garden features, the pool is the most difficult to change once it is in place and filled with water.

EXCAVATING

Use pegs to mark an outline 25–30cm (10–12in) outside the outline of the pool and remove the canes. Excavate a hole to the depth of the liner, plus 5–7.5cm (2–3in) in all directions. Remember, too, to allow for the ledges or ridges within the pool. This may involve taking the pool liner in and out of the hole until you get the contours absolutely right. Add a layer of sand 5–7.5cm (2–3in) deep in the bottom of the hole. Carefully place the liner on the sand so that the lip of the pool is flush with the surrounding soil surface. You may need to add or remove some sand.

Use a spirit level laid on a long plank to check that the pool is absolutely level in all directions. If you do not do this you will forever have the frustration of a pool with a greater depth to the water surface at one end than the other. Pour sand around the pool to fill the gap between the sides of the pool and the sides of the holes, tamping it down carefully so that there are no pockets of air. Check again that the pool is perfectly level. This is your last opportunity to adjust the position of the pool before you fill it with water.

EDGING

The next step is to provide some form of edging to the pool so that the surrounding soil does not fall in. You can use either regular stone slabs, which create a semi-formal pool, or irregularly arranged slabs, which will allow you to introduce more natural-looking planting. Whichever you choose, it is important to use mortar to provide a rigid and secure edge. The edging stones or slabs should overhang the water, both to disguise the edge of the liner and to protect the lip of the liner from direct sunlight.

If you have selected a pool liner with trough-type ledges around the edges, you can fill these with soil for planting. If, as is usually the case, they are simply shelves, you will have to secure all your marginal plants within baskets before you place them in the pool.

BUILDING A WATER GARDEN –

In many respects, flexible liners are the ideal material to use for creating pools, whether your preference is for formal or informal, large or small, raised or sunken. Flexible liners are suitable for pools of all sizes, and the shape is limited only by the size of your own garden and your imagination. Unlike pre-formed pools, some of which are still being made in rather bright colours – swimming pool blue seems to be a favourite – flexible liners, both **PVC** and butyl, are black or occasionally dark green or dark brown, colours which are much more sympathetic in all situations and can be disguised successfully. In addition, the positions of the ledges and the various depths within the pool can be a matter of personal choice, allowing you to plan the pool with specific plant types in mind. Finally, a flexible liner allows you to create a pool that is deep enough to accommodate fish. A pre-formed pool may not be deep enough for fish to survive really cold winters.

CHOOSING A LINER

Before you buy a liner, make sure that you buy one that has been specially made for pool use. Normal polyethyl-

Stone slabs can be used as a border to edge a pool

FLEXIBLE LINERS

ene sheeting, no matter how thick, is simply not good enough. It does not have the correct flexibility and stretching properties, it is easily punctured and torn, and it will deteriorate when it is exposed to sunlight. As a temporary measure, you could use a double layer of 500 gauge sheeting, but this will not last for more than two or three years.

Polyvinyl chloride (PVC) is a much better material. It is stronger than ordinary polyethylene and is more durable and relatively cheap. If you choose a PVC liner, look for one that is guaranteed for at least 10 years.

Best of all, however, is butyl rubber, which is a synthetic, flexible, rubber-like material, which is normally guaranteed for about 20 years but should last considerably longer. Butyl is, however, the most expensive of the available materials. Whether you choose PVC or butyl, buy a liner that is at least 0.6mm thick; ideally, the liner should be 0.8–1mm thick.

USING A FLEXIBLE LINER

Mark out the shape of your pool on the ground. You will find that laying a flexible hosepipe or length of rope on the ground is the easiest way to indicate the outline of the pool. Sand, which stands out well on grass and can be 'dispensed' from an empty soft-drinks bottle, can also be used, but it is more difficult to change the outlines. Rope or hosepipe can simply be picked up and moved, but sand must be scuffed out and reapplied.

As well as allowing you to work out the dimensions of the materials you will need, this initial outline will enable you to assess the proposed position of the pool from your patio or house and from other parts of the garden. Although informal pools will have curved edges, too many small indentations will be difficult to line successfully and will not look natural.

EXCAVATING

When you are satisfied with the position and overall outline you can begin to dig the hole. Make sure that you introduce ledges of different depths on which planting baskets can stand, and make a shallow ledge, about 20cm (8in) all round the edge, for marginal plants. The depth of your pond will depend on several factors, especially the type of subsoil you find as you dig down and on the water table in your garden. Bear in mind, however, that the greater the volume of water in the pool, the easier it is to maintain a good balance of aquatic organisms and to ensure that the water remains clear. The minimum depth to which you should dig, therefore, is 45cm (18in).

CALCULATIONS

Measure a rectangle that will encompass the size and shape of the pool you have excavated. Add to both width and length a figure representing twice the depth of the pond at its deepest point and then allow an additional 45cm (18in) to both dimensions for a flap all around the circumference. If, for example, your pool would fit into a rectangle measuring 3m (10ft) by 2m (6ft) and the hole was 45cm (18in) deep, you would need a liner measuring at least 3 + 0.90 + 0.45m (4.35m) by 2 + 0.90 + 0.45m (3.35m). If you are planning an associated bog garden or if you have introduced a ridge across the bottom of the pool or if the sides are sharply vertical, you will need extra liner. If you are in any doubt, use a length of rope or a piece of string to measure both dimensions, allowing the rope or string to follow the contours you have excavated, and remember to add on sufficient for the flap.

LAYING THE LINER

Before you lay the liner you will need to protect it. Remove any stones from the bottom and sides of the pool. If the subsoil is very stony and contains builder's rubble, add a layer of sand to the bottom of the pool. Next, add some protective material – just as you would place an underlay under a new carpet. Commercially made polyester lining material will be available from the same sources as the pool liner itself, and if you want a durable, non-leaking pool, it is worth the additional expense. Old synthetic carpet may be a cheaper alternative, as may insulation felting. Some people suggest using layers of newspaper, but the paper will eventually rot away and may allow stones to puncture the liner and should be avoided for this reason.

When laying the flexible liner, you will find it easier if you have some help. Lay the liner loosely over the hole. If you are using PVC, it is sometimes easier to work with if you are able to stretch it out in the sun so that it becomes more flexible. When in place, lay stones or bricks all around the edge of the liner so that it is temporarily anchored, and begin to pour water slowly into the centre of the liner with a hosepipe. A butyl liner will

BUILDING A WATER GARDEN –

The real skill in water garden construction lies in making it appear natural

FLEXIBLE LINERS

gradually stretch to fill the contours of the pool, so you must move the rocks holding it down to take account of this characteristic.

When the pool is almost full, trim the liner so there is an even flap all the way round. If you are adding an edging of paving stones or bricks, the flap need be no more than 20cm (8in). Surround the pool with paving slabs or bricks set in concrete as for a formal pool or more irregularly shaped stones for a more informal one. Fill the gaps between the rocks with soil to create areas that can be filled with waterside plants. As with pre-formed pools, it is important that the edging stones overhang the pool so that the liner is both hidden from view and protected from the damaging effects of sunlight. Even the best quality liners will wear out more quickly if they are continually exposed to the sun.

A FORMAL, RAISED POOL

Butyl liners can also be used to create a raised or partially raised pool in a formal or courtyard garden. On a patio a raised pool can provide an attractive focal point and, if the edge is securely capped by paving stones, an extra seating area.

Constructing such a pool, however, requires far greater building skills than does the creation of an informal pool excavated in garden soil, and is likely to be more expensive to build. The pressure exerted by water in a pool that is 40–45cm (16–18in) above ground is so great that you will need a double wall of bricks to contain the liner. You will also need to excavate a trench to contain the foundation rows of bricks and to make provision for an overflow pipe.

A raised pool with a liner instead of a rigid, pre-formed pool can be any shape you wish, and this is probably the approach to adopt if you want a circular pool or a geometric shape such as a hexagon or octagon on your patio or as the centrepiece of a courtyard. The outside of the pool should be faced with bricks or stones that are in keeping with the remainder of the hard landscaping around it. The planting in such a pool should be limited to just a few species, although you should not forget to include oxygenators and, if you wish, goldfish.

With ingenuity and careful construction, pools can be raised above the level of the surrounding garden

BUILDING A WATER GARDEN –

The advent of pre-formed pools and butyl liners has tended to make the building of pools from concrete a less common option, but if you want a formal pool, do consider using concrete, as it is a durable, strong material with a good, watertight finish. Making a concrete pool is not an easy undertaking, however, and it requires far more building expertise than using a liner or a pre-formed pool. Remember, too, that once built, a concrete pool will be difficult to get rid of if you decide you do not like it or find it is in the wrong place.

Make a simple pool more interesting by adding well thought-out features

PLANNING

Check that ground on which you are going to put the pool is completely stable. If it is not, you may have to bed the pool into a layer of compacted hardcore. For an informal pool, the deepest part of the pool, where the fish and water lilies will be, should be a rectangle or square, and it should have sides that slope outwards at an angle of about 20 degrees to reduce the pressure exerted as ice expands in winter, which is a common cause of cracks. The rest of the pool, including the planting ledges, can be any shape you wish, but add at least an additional 15cm (6in) to the depth and to all the sides – this is the minimum thickness of concrete that will be necessary to make a strong pool. In a formal pool, where it is more likely that you will want the sides to be completely vertical, you should be prepared to make the concrete about 20cm (8in) thick.

The larger the pool, the more important it is that you include heavy gauge wire mesh or reinforcing steel mesh, and it is vital that the concrete completely fills the holes and that there are no spaces left around the mesh. A very large pool will need steel reinforcing rods.

The most problematic part of building a large, formal, concrete pool is the need for shuttering, which is used to hold the concrete in place while it sets. Without shuttering, there is a danger that the concrete will slide down the walls, so that they are thinner at the top but bulging at the bottom. The shuttering, which is a bottomless, topless box made of wood and smaller in all dimensions by the thickness of the concrete, is built inside the pool when the base has been completed.

BUILDING THE POOL

Make the bottom of the pool first by laying poured concrete over a layer of hardcore. Include wire mesh between two layers of concrete, and leave to set. The shuttering must be built in situ so that it is both completely rigid and easily taken apart. Build the shuttering and insert mesh in the sides and then add the concrete. When the concrete is dry remove the shuttering and coat the sides and base of the pool with a proprietary waterproof sealant.

If the mix was wrong in some way – the proportions of the cement, sand and aggregate were wrong – or if the materials were not thoroughly mixed together before water was added, the pool will leak. Cracks may also occur if the foundations subside.

Ready-mixed concrete is easy to work with and will have been made to the correct consistency. Its main drawback is that everything must be absolutely ready so that the concrete is used on the day it is delivered. You should also think about access and how you will transport your load of concrete from where it is delivered to

CONCRETE-LINED POOLS

the site of the pool. If you decide to mix your own concrete, which is possible to do if you are building a small pool, it is vital that you get the proportions right. Use good quality cement, sharp builder's sand and clean gravel or ballast (aggregate) in the proportions 1:2:3 by volume (not weight). Do not add too much water, leaving puddles in the mix: your aim is to get a smooth consistency. Add a waterproofing agent, which will increase the durability and impermeability of the concrete. Using a concrete mixer, which can be hired by the day, will make sure the concrete is thoroughly mixed and will keep it workable for you.

REPAIRING A CONCRETE POND

Poured concrete is, sadly, prone to cracking. Even if you do not build your own pond with concrete, you may inherit such a pond in a new garden, and should you discover your pond leaks, it is at least possible to effect short-term repairs.

Once you have found the crack, use a thin stone chisel and a club hammer to widen it. Tap very slowly and gently. Clean away all the debris with a stiff brush. Mix the mortar and use a trowel to fill the crack. Leave it to dry for at least 48 hours. Apply a coat of a proprietary pool sealant to the crack to prevent toxins from leaking into the water.

This will not be a very long-lasting solution to the leak, and you may eventually find it necessary to line the pool with a butyl liner.

Nothing is more frustrating than a really mature pool that springs a leak

31

BUILDING A WATER GARDEN –

Puddled clay was probably the first material to be used in the construction of ponds, and advocates of the truly natural pool would say that it is still the most appropriate material and the most environmentally friendly. Such pools used to be called dew pools, probably because night dew contributed to the water content, and it is thought that they were originally built as a means of providing water for farm stock.

In the late 19th century clay was used to make a few pools for ornamental gardens, but it must have been a very messy business. After the hole had been excavated, it was lined with soot to deter worms and other burrowing creatures. This was then covered with a layer of straw or heather, depending on what local materials were available. This in turn was covered with a layer of clay. The clay had to be kept damp while it was worked and kneaded into the straw, and it was pressed into place with rollers or, in country areas, horses were used to trample it down. It would then be filled with water. Dew accumulating on the cold clay and water that leaked from land drains were usually sufficient to keep it topped up.

LINING

Lining a pool with clay is enormously hard work, and unless you are a purist and have plenty of energy, a clay pool is probably not for you. However, it is possible and, with today's modern materials, a little easier than it was in the past.

The first point to bear in mind is that the hole you excavate is going to be lined with a layer of clay that must be at least 15cm (6in) thick and that this will, in turn, be covered with a layer of soil, so take this into account when you are planning the pool and before you begin digging. The second point to consider is that the surface of the clay will be damaged by vigorous tree roots extending into it. Construct the pond well away from trees that might cause future problems. Third, clay linings work best on gradually sloping pool sides. It is not a suitable material if you want a pool with steep sides. It is essential that a clay-lined pond is kept filled with water, otherwise the clay dries, cracks and leaks.

Clay can usually be obtained from builder's merchants if your own soil is unsuitable, but it is worth carrying out a quick test to see if the clay content of your garden is suitable. Sift some soil into a screw-top jar and add some water and a pinch of salt. Shake the jar, then leave for at least two days. The sediment at the bottom of the jar will be sand, while organic matter will be floating on top. The layer in middle will be clay, and if it represents about 60 per cent of the whole, your soil should be suitable for puddling.

Whether you use clay from your own garden or have a quantity delivered from a builder's merchant, excavate the hole, allowing for the additional thickness of the layer of clay, and remove all stones and roots. Protect the clay by scattering soot over the surface of the hole, and then begin to apply the clay. If it is a fairly small pool, you may be able to do this by hand or with the aid of wooden paddles or 'tampers'. If your pool is large, it is worth hiring special mechanical rollers. The clay must be kept wet at all times, so you may have to set up your garden sprinkler or to cover the areas you have finished with damp hessian or sacks. Be warned, this job is neither easy or clean! When you have covered the surface with clay and before it dries out, cover the clay with a layer of garden soil to a depth of at least 15cm (6in) and slowly begin to fill the pool with water.

ALTERNATIVES

An alternative and easier approach is to use bentonite, a type of clay which is derived from volcanic ash. It has many of the same properties as fuller's earth and is used to line reservoirs and canals. Available from specialist suppliers, it comes in two forms: either as crystals or as matting. When the crystals are mixed with water, a water-resistant gel is produced. This should be applied all over the surface of the pool. A layer of soil is then added so that the gel is completely covered.

Easier still than the bentonite crystals is a relatively new material, known as bentomat, which is based on layers of geotextile with bentonite crystals between the layers. This material, can be laid in much the same way as butyl liner but, like traditional clay, it must be covered with a layer of soil of about 30cm (12in) deep. When the pool is filled, the water penetrates through the geotextile and causes the bentonite crystals to swell and bond together, thus forming an impermeable barrier.

CLAY-LINED POOLS

Whatever method of clay you use to line your pond, it is advisable to keep all water plants in baskets to contain their roots. The questing roots of vigorous water lilies, for example, planted directly into the soil in the base of the pool, will quickly penetrate the clay. Moreover, if you need to remove or divide plants that have rooted themselves in the clay, you will damage the surface as you remove them, causing leaks.

A clay liner probably does create the ultimate natural pool but it is very tricky to get right

WATER GARDEN MAINTENANCE

The water garden has fewer potential problems than almost any other area of the garden. The number of pests and diseases that can affect the plants is limited, and there is, in any case, little that you can do, beyond removing dead and damaged leaves. Chemical sprays cannot, of course, be used in a pond.

EMPTYING AND CLEANING THE POOL

From time to time it may be necessary to empty your pool – the water may be polluted or the pool may be leaking, for example, or their may be a very deep layer of silt and soil in the bottom. It is not worth tying to keep the bottom of your pool entirely free of silt because a certain amount is inevitable, but the decay and putrefaction that result from the build-up of water plants and leaves from nearby deciduous trees and shrubs can upset the balance of the pool if it is not checked. Although autumn or winter may seem to be appropriate times to empty and clean out a pool, these are the very times when the pool water should be left undisturbed. Many plants produce buds, which will flourish the following spring but which will spend the winter in the bottom of the pool, and lifting and disturbing them in winter may harm them. A mild spring day is the best time to empty the pool.

Take all the marginal plants and deep-water aquatics out of the pool. Keep some of the best plants, dividing those that are crowded in their baskets and discarding the overgrown centres. Take the opportunity to throw away the old soil and to replace it all with new. Mix some bonemeal

Emptying and cleaning a pool isn't something to be undertaken unless it is absolutely necessary

with the growing medium. Stand the plants in water or find some other way of keeping them wet while you finish the pool.

Remove the fish to a holding pool – a plastic bowl will do – but make sure it is filled with water from the pool. As you take out each fish, check it quickly for signs of disease. Take out the oxygenators and any floating plants and put them in a bucket, checking that there are no fish hidden among the mass of vegetation. If you have a submersible pump in the pond, connect it to a hose so that the water is pumped away; otherwise, you will have to siphon the water out. You will probably have to scoop out the water from the very bottom of the pool with a bowl. Keep a watch for frogs and newts.

If the pool is made with a butyl liner, work very carefully as you remove the silt to ensure that you do not cause any damage. The discarded silt should be put on the compost heap when you are sure there are no hidden creatures in it. Hose the pool clean, sweeping over the surface with a brush. If you have a pre-formed pool, scrub it, using a mild disinfectant or sufficient permanganate of potash to turn the water pink. Rinse, leave to dry and then replant.

REPAIRING LEAKS

If a concrete pool has been made with wrong type of sand or if the materials were not mixed together properly, a network of fine cracks may appear on the surface. Applying two coats of a proprietary pond sealant should help, but make sure the sealant covers not only the cracks but an area well beyond them. Repairing a larger crack is discussed on p.31. Eventually, it may be necessary to line a leaking concrete pool with a butyl liner.

Butyl liners do not crack, of course, but they are vulnerable to sharp objects, both in the form of stones working through the soil or being forced upwards by the movement of the land, or in the form of carelessly handled forks or secateurs. If the water in a pool constructed with a butyl liner always needs topping up leading you to suspect that the liner is damaged, it will be necessary to empty out the water. Finding the leak may not be easy but it can be repaired with one of the proprietary kits that are available from the suppliers of liners or from the larger garden centres.

Keep plants in buckets then re-plant a week after re-filling the pool

WATER GARDEN MAINTENANCE

Allow the water temperature of the pool and the bag to equilibrate

Pre-formed pools will crack if they are subjected to unequal pressure, such as happens if they are not perfectly level when they are installed. Again, repair kits containing a type of fibreglass matting are available from specialist aquatic suppliers.

CARING FOR POOL PLANTS

Even if you have a natural pool and are using mostly indigenous plant species, do not plant aquatic species directly into the soil and silt in the bottom of the pool. If you do, the larger, more vigorous plants, especially the water lilies, will swamp the smaller species and it will be very difficult to remove individual plants as the roots will become tangled up with each other. Aquatic plants should be planted into individual baskets so that water and the gases in the water can circulate freely around the plants' roots but the roots are contained. Most garden centres will offer a wide range of planting baskets specially designed for water plants. Some are curved, so that they fit snugly against the sides of pre-formed pools, but most are round or square. Although some newer types of planting basket have fine mesh sides, most have fairly open sides, and the baskets have to be lined so that the soil does not wash directly into the pool before the plants' roots have grown to bind the soil in place. The best material for this lining is sacking or hessian. Place a large piece of hessian in the basket and use good quality garden soil to fill the basket. When the root is in place, tuck the hessian over the top to stop the soil spilling out, and add a layer about 2.5cm (1in) deep of clean, washed shingle. Not only will the shingle keep the soil from floating away, but it will also prevent fish from rooting about in the soil.

When you are cleaning the pond in spring, take the opportunity to lift and divide water plants before they start into growth; this should be done to any plants that have been in place for four years or more. Lift out the baskets and carefully remove the shingle. Wash the roots and cut away the old parts of the tuber, retaining the eyes (plants with small leaves). Make sure that the tuber does not dry out as you are working on it. Replant young pieces of tuber that are about 15cm (6in) in size and that have a strong shoot growing from them. Use new, fresh loam and add some bonemeal to the planting medium.

ADDING FISH

Do not introduce fish to your pool for at least two weeks, ideally three or four weeks, after planting. This will give the water time to achieve a balance. Buy your fish from a reputable supplier in late spring or early summer. Check each fish as you choose it, looking closely for signs of disease. Erect dorsal fins are usually a good indication, as are bright, well-set eyes. Never buy a fish that has any white spots on it. Transport the fish in polythene bags that are inflated with additional air. If they are in good condition, the fish should survive in these bags for at least 24 hours if kept in a cool place.

Float the polythene bags on the pool's surface for about an hour; the aim is gradually to equalize the temperature of the water in the polythene bag with that of the water in the pool. Open the polythene bag and add some pool water. Leave again for 15 minutes or so before allowing the fish to slip into the pool. They will probably disappear to the bottom of the pool and hide among the plants for several days.

CLEARING ICE

Part of the pool surface must be kept free of ice in order for gas exchange to take place. Without this, fish will die. Some people recommend floating a ball or piece of expanded polystyrene in the pool, although this is not always successful. The most effective way of keeping the water thawed is to use a small, low-voltage floating heater. If you have a fountain, keeping it running continually will, in most periods of cold weather, keep the surface free of ice, but carefully pouring hot water into one corner will do just as well. Another solution is to stand a flat-bottomed saucepan or casserole dish filled with very hot water on the ice. Unless the ice is very thick, this should be sufficient to make a hole. Never, ever use a hammer to smash the ice on a pool if there are fish in it. The resulting shock waves will probably kill the fish.

Any still water pool is almost bound to freeze during the winter

TYPES OF WATER GARDEN PLANT

All plants, even desert species, require moisture in order to grow but my interest in this book is in those that require rather more than an average amount of water in the environment. There is a range of species that can be most usefully grouped according to how wet are the conditions that they prefer.

At the greatest extreme are the **submerged plants** (see pp.74–81) that live entirely or almost entirely submerged, sometimes hardly rooted in the pool mud and emerging above the water surface, if at all, only to flower. They might be thought scarcely worthy of cultivation but, in reality, are among the most important pool plants because oxygen diffuses from their leaves into the water and thus they benefit other plants, fish and other forms of water life. Nonetheless, in saying this, I am merely repeating conventional wisdom for I have found that it is on and around the submerged plants that much troublesome blanket weed develops (see p.43), and I have had very successful garden pools that contained no oxygenating plants at all and in which the oxygenating role was completely taken over by the pool fountain.

Floating plants (see pp.82–7) are those that, believe it or not, simply float. Some have no roots, some have roots that dangle into the water, but none are anchored in any way. They die down in the winter to survive as dormant buds, resting in the mud of the pool floor to grow and rise again with the arrival of warmer conditions in the spring. Many species of floating plant multiply vegetatively with great rapidity and, in consequence, can cause serious problems if they are allowed into rivers, canals or other water courses, as they can cause severe blockages. For this reason, their sale may be restricted in some warmer climates where the mild winter offers less of a check to their development.

The group that I have called simply **water plants** (see pp.60–73) are those that grow within the pool, anchored in the mud but with leaves and flowers arising to float at the surface or to rise above it. Water lilies are the classic water plants and they exemplify one of the most important features of the group, in that the depth of water to which they are most suited and the vigour of their surface spread varies considerably between varieties, which must, therefore, be chosen carefully.

Plants that grow at the very edge of the water are called **marginals** (see pp.44–59). The group covers a wide range of habitat requirements, from those species that must exist permanently in several centimetres of water through those that tolerate periodic drying out of the water's edge, to those that need saturated, waterlogged soil but not actually standing

A pool featuring a good collection of water and marginal plants

water. The marginals will grade almost imperceptibly into the plants of the **bog garden** (see pp.88–91). This is the most varied habitat, for at one extreme are the plants that are only one step removed from the marginals that need very wet soil, while at the other end there are those species that require moisture-retentive soil but which are intolerant of waterlogging. A number would be described simply as border perennials but I have included them here for I believe that the more informal type of water garden, which often includes a bog garden, should grade gradually into other, drier parts of the garden. Which part of the bog garden is most appropriate for each species is important: check when buying if the plants require high, moderate or low soil moisture.

A well-filled garden can contain a wide range of different water-loving plants

PLANTING, FEEDING AND AFTERCARE

By and large, water plants require rather less routine care and attention than almost any other type of garden plant. With one or two possible exceptions among some barely hardy, floating forms, none of them are grown as annuals so there is no routine raising and renewal of plants to consider. I have given notes on propagation for each species because it may be necessary, from time to time, to increase or renew your stock but it is never an annual chore. Indeed, in a number of cases, limiting propagation is more the order of the day because, as a group, water plants include a disproportionate number of vigorous forms.

For the various groups that actually grow within the water of the pool, planting is simplicity itself: for most submerged and floating plants, the operation comprises merely dropping them into the water. Attaching a small weight to a clump of shoots may be necessary for those submerged types that are to take root in the mud at the pool bottom. Water plants and marginals may be planted directly into the mud or into planting baskets containing soil, which are lowered or placed into the chosen spot. Once handmade of wicker, these baskets are now manufactured in moulded plastic and are sold in various sizes, appropriate for different sizes of plant. Planting into a basket overcomes the difficulty (and sometimes danger) of trying to plant into the deep water of an established pool but it also has the advantages of

Decorative water plants grown in baskets add variety and colour

allowing plants to be lifted for periodic division or renewal and, most importantly, of limiting the spread of particularly invasive marginal species when grown in restricted spaces. When planting baskets are to be placed within the pool, it is important to place a layer of about 3cm (1½in) of clean grit over the soil surface and around the crown of the plant otherwise fish will disturb the soil and easily uproot the plants from their settled positions.

Whether the plants are planted into baskets, directly into ledges within the pool or at the pool edge, it is essential to use soil to which no organic matter or fertilizer has been added, as this will both foul the water and encourage the growth of blanket weed and other algae. Soil from a relatively neglected part of the garden is ideal. Feeding water garden plants is simple; purpose-made sachets of specially formulated fertilizer are available for placing beneath the water plants at planting time, but I have never used these and have never found them necessary. The only water garden plants that I do feed are those in the bog garden which I feed in exactly the same way as, but to a rather lesser degree than, border perennials, giving a light dressing of general fertilizer, such as fish blood and bone in the spring. I also mulch them in autumn and spring, for even bog gardens can become drier during the summer, and it is the spring mulch which is intended to keep the roots fully moist, while the autumn mulch will offer protection from any penetrating winter frosts. Whenever possible, however, I do use composts rather than animal manures when mulching bog garden plants.

There are few water-garden perennials that require staking and notes on any cutting back or pruning necessary are given under the individual descriptions. But I must repeat that, by and large, water garden plants are little trouble.

PROPAGATION

Almost without exception, the water plants in this book are perennials. But as I often find myself having to explain, perennial does not equate with immortal and so, at times, you will need to replenish your stock. And I say replenish rather than replace for even an old and overgrown plant can often be rescued by knowing how it is best propagated. Whichever method you select, you will almost certainly find yourself with more plants than you need but you can share them with friends. I find that this is something especially appreciated with water plants since nurseries and garden centres tend to restrict themselves to a limited range of species and varieties. If you have something unusual, what better way for it to become better known than for you to propagate and distribute it?

DIVISION

The simplest method of propagation, and the one applicable to most types of water plant, is by division — the practice of splitting an existing plant into several smaller parts. Apart from some of the hardier bog garden species, much the best time to divide is in the spring, as the air, soil and water are beginning to warm up but before growth has really started. Dig up the plant, or lift it if it is in a planting basket. The old basket should be cut away and disposed of and the clump split by whatever means is appropriate. Discard the old, congested parts of the plant from the centre and only replant the small, younger vigorous pieces from the periphery.

CUTTINGS

I find only two types of cutting are of value in the propagation of water plants: stem cuttings (those that with normal terrestrial plants would be called softwood or semi-ripe cuttings) and, sometimes, leaf-bud cuttings. Hormone rooting powder may be used with all of them.

All cuttings should be rooted in either a propagator or a covered cold-frame. It is very important to maintain a moist atmosphere around all cuttings. Use a hand sprayer to mist over the cuttings regularly. The effectiveness of the type of medium into which the cuttings are placed varies from one type of plant to another and I have given my suggestions in the individual descriptions.

Stem cuttings should be about 15cm (6in) long, be removed from the parent plant with a clean cut made just below a bud and the large leaves trimmed off. They should be inserted to a depth of approximately 5cm (2in) in the rooting medium. Leaf-bud cuttings should comprise a leaf with adjoining bud and about 1cm (½in) of stem either side. They should be inserted so that the bud is below the surface of the rooting medium.

SEED

Many types of water plant *can* be raised from seed although it has to be said that many perennial forms are selected varieties that give rise to rather variable offspring when multiplied in this way and are indeed better propagated by cuttings, or bought as named plants. I have indicated in the text where this is so. The few annual species of course must be raised from seed and this can be done either directly outdoors ('the hardy annual technique') or into a seedling compost under protection (the 'half-hardy annual technique'), the seedling then being hardened-off before planting out.

Sowing seeds and raising seedlings on the greenhouse bench or even on the kitchen window ledge is not only easy, it is also very satisfying. You will require a compost in which to sow the seed, a propagator in which to put the compost, water, in most instances light and a means of supplying an adequate temperature. The compost should be at least based on a proprietary mixture, either soil-based or soilless but often with the addition of some sand. Always use fresh compost for each batch of seeds.

Generally, seeds require a slightly higher temperature in order to germinate than the plants ever require again. Moreover, within fairly well defined limits for each type of seed, the higher the temperature the more rapid and uniform the germination. Provision of an adequate and appropriate temperature is thus very important and as the seed of some water plants can be somewhat stubborn in germinating, it is worth giving a little attention to providing the correct temperature. Once germinated and hardened-off, grow on perennial species in pots, which must be kept constantly moist, feeding them in the meantime, and then planted out, in the following year.

OTHER POOL LIFE

The first animals that most people think of when they consider stocking a pool are, of course, fish, but many water creatures will arrive of their own accord. There is little you can do to make sure that frogs and newts will find your pool appealing, but if they do happen to come along, they should be welcomed.

A pool is the only part of the garden in which snails are welcome, for the aquatic species are not damaging to plant life in the same way as their terrestrial relatives. They have some value as scavengers in feeding on dead plant material but, contrary to what is sometimes suggested, they will not help to control algal growth and 'green water'. Although you can buy water snails of various types from specialist water garden suppliers, they will inevitably be introduced on water plants and as eggs adhering to birds' feet. It is often said that the common pond snail is more damaging to water plants than the rather more attractive flat-shelled ram's horn snail, but in reality the ram's horn snail seems less well adapted to pool life than its common cousin and may die out in time.

If you have a large pool or even a lake, ducks and other water fowl may be attracted to it. Dragonflies and damselflies are the most spectacular of the insects that you will see, although countless others will appear, both in and above the water. Some gardeners are worried by the small, wriggling creatures that appear in their pools. Most are insect larvae but many things in pools wriggle, although none of them need cause any concern.

FISH

Many people feel that fish have no place in a natural or wildlife pool. If you would like fish, however, you must select them carefully, not only in terms of the type that is most appropriate for the sort of pool you have but also to make sure that they are of the correct size and quantity.

If you want to aspire to choice selections such as koi, you need to create pools and conditions specially designed for them.

In most garden pools, however, koi are inappropriate. Not only will they uproot plants and cause general mayhem, but they will also require protection from herons as well as potential thieves, for fine specimens are very valuable. This need for protection – netting, alarms and scaring devices – makes koi the choice of enthusiasts only.

More appropriate in ornamental pools are goldfish and their multi-coloured relatives, shubunkins, which can be combined with a few slender golden orfe and some golden rudd. Carp are too large and too damaging for plant life in garden pools, and minnows should be kept only in a large pool that also has constantly moving water.

Buy fish that are about 10cm (4in) in length. The number is likely to be critical only in a small pool, when 12–20 fish is about right. Do not introduce fish until about three weeks after the plants have had a chance to settle down. At first they will disappear to the deeper water for about two weeks. When they begin to appear on the surface, offer a proprietary floating fish food, following the manufacturer's recommendations on amount and frequency.

Fish and water lilies together create the traditional image of a pond

PROBLEMS

One of the great advantages of water plants is that they are relatively free from problems caused by pests and diseases. There is, in any case, little that can be done about any problems that do arise because fungicidal and pesticidal sprays cannot be used in the water garden because of the harm they will do to the other pool inhabitants.

PESTS

Aphids are the commonest pests in the water garden, and they are most easily disposed of by being washed off the plants with a jet of water from a hosepipe, when they will fall into the water and be eaten by the fish.

Water lilies are affected by a wider range of pests and diseases than almost any other water garden plant, although few are serious. The exception is the water lily beetle, a small, brown beetle with small, brown larvae, both of which eat out holes and furrows in the upper surface of the leaves, not only disfiguring them but, more importantly, also allowing fungal decay to take hold. Insecticidal control is not an option, and once again treatment consists of using the hosepipe to wash off the beetles and vigilance so that prompt action can be taken at the first sign of symptoms.

DISEASES

Fungal leaf spots are the commonest disease problem, and seriously affected leaves should be cut off and disposed of. Mildew can be troublesome on some marginal and water garden plants, but it tends not to be serious until temperatures rise in summer. Provided this happens after flowering, the plants can be partially cut back and the seriously affected foliage taken away.

WATER CLARITY

The greatest problems facing a garden pool are likely to be green 'slime' and green 'pea soup' water. Both problems are algal in origin. Green slime is a growth of filamentous green algae, known as blanket weed, while soupy water results from the build up of vast populations of microscopic, single-celled green algae in a process sometimes called 'blooming'.

It has been suggested that submerged oxygenating plants, especially *Elodea*, encourage blanket weed by providing it with a base on which to grow. Check all new plant introductions for signs of blanket weed and reject them if you are in any doubt. Some people suggest that filling a pool with rainwater rather than with tapwater reduces algal growth because it contains fewer of the chemicals that algae use as a source of nitrogen. Whatever water you use, it is important to prevent any run-off of fertilizer from adjoining parts of the garden. Containers standing near the pool edge are common offenders – always move them away from the water's edge when applying liquid feed.

Using proprietary algicidal chemicals to the water once blanket weed is established will kill it and may even do so without harming the other life in the pool, but the result will be a layer of dead blanket weed, which will decompose and create even more problems. The best method of control is to remove the weed by hand or by twisting it around a wooden forked stick. Never use a rake or fork if you have a pool with a flexible liner. Put the weed in an old container to allow small fish and newts to escape before you discard the weed. Placing nets filled with barley or lavender straw in the water also helps control the weed.

Both mechanical and biological filters are available. Mechanical filters pump water through a pad that removes particles, including green algae. The filters are small, submersible and unobtrusive, and the same pump can operate the fountain. Biological filters pump water through bacteria-containing layers. The bacteria digest the waste organic matter and algae, turning it into harmless material. The pump may be submerged, but the filter is in a box that must be hidden. Ultraviolet water clarifiers pass the water through a chamber in which it is exposed to UV rays, which kill the algal cells.

Use all these methods routinely.

Water lilies can suffer from severe aphid infestation

MARGINALS

Acorus calamus Sweet flag

"This is an odd plant and no mistake, looking for all the world like one of the irises and sharing one of their common names, flag. But the affinities of this native of Asia and North America (although widely naturalized in Europe) are with arums and their kin. History relates that the foliage was used to cover the floors of castles before carpets, and it would have made a good choice, for the 'sweet' epithet of the common name alludes to the pleasant aroma, variously described as of citrus or cinnamon, that exudes from the bruised leaves. An oil used in perfumery is also extracted from the rhizome of the plant."

FLOWERS Insignificant, greenish-brown in arum-like spikes borne towards the tops of the stems. In warm areas, reddish fruits are formed but these do not occur in Britain.
FOLIAGE Deciduous, iris-like, up to 2.5cm (1in) wide, usually wrinkled and with pronounced mid-rib.
SITE Full sun or very light shade.
PREFERRED WATER DEPTH 8–25cm (3–10in) (rather less than half this for A. gramineus which prefers shallower depths).
RECOMMENDED POOL SIZE Medium (A. calamus) or small (A. gramineus).
SPECIAL REQUIREMENTS None.
HARDINESS Very hardy, tolerating -20°C (-4°F).
SIZE Will attain 1.25 x 75cm (4ft x 30in) after five years; A. gramineus, less than half this.

PLANTING
As rhizomes in spring, directly into the soil.
CARE
Cut down dead foliage and flower spike in autumn or, alternatively, in colder areas, in spring.
PROPAGATION
By division in spring.
PROBLEMS
None.

RECOMMENDED VARIETIES
'Variegatus' has gold and cream-striped leaves, less significant flowers and is slower and more compact in growth.

Acorus calamus

SIMILAR SPECIES
Acorus gramineus (Japanese rush – another misnomer) is a smaller, neater plant with almost grass-like leaves, which also exists in a variegated form, 'Variegatus', sometimes seen as a houseplant.

Alisma plantago-aquatica Water plantain

"As its common name suggests, the foliage of Alisma does indeed look like that of a plantain that has somehow become lost and ended up in a pool. The appearance of the flowers, however, confirms that there is no relationship with real plantains; nor indeed is there any with Gypsophila, which is what the feathery blossom most suggests. Alismas should be planted with caution for they can self-seed with wicked abandon. In a wilder garden, the seedheads are welcome as bird food but in smaller, more kempt surroundings, the flower spikes are best cut back before the seeds are set, so as to limit the spread. The entire plant has an acrid smell and can be poisonous; certainly a sedative drug was formerly extracted from the roots."

PLANTING
As plants in spring, directly into soil in large pools or in planting baskets.
CARE
Cut down dead flower spikes immediately after flowering in all except

large, wild gardens and cut back dead foliage in autumn.

PROPAGATION
By division in spring, or by seed (most readily by the removal of self-sown seedlings).

PROBLEMS
None.

FLOWERS Small, white, pink or purplish in large, feathery inflorescences.
FOLIAGE Deciduous, plantain-like, broadly elliptical on stalks emerging above water surface.
SITE Full sun.
PREFERRED WATER DEPTH 15–25cm (6–10in) (approximately half of this for *A. lanceolatum*).
RECOMMENDED POOL SIZE Large or medium.
SPECIAL REQUIREMENTS None.
HARDINESS Very hardy, tolerating -20°C (-4°F).
SIZE Will attain 75 x 45cm (30 x 18in) after two or three years; *A. lanceolatum*, rather less.

SIMILAR SPECIES
Alisma lanceolatum is smaller with narrower, more grass-like foliage.

RECOMMENDED VARIETIES
Normal species is usually the only form available although var. *parviflorum* is sometimes seen; it is much smaller, with smaller, pink flowers.

Butomus umbellatus Flowering rush

❝ Like so many water plants, this one also has a common name that serves to mislead. It isn't a rush and even if it were, so what, for they have flowers too. I wish it was called the umbrella plant as that would more accurately convey its appearance as the stately flower stems arise above the water surface; but the name umbrella plant is already in use for several other things. ❞

PLANTING
As plants in spring, directly into soil in large pools or in planting baskets.

CARE
Cut down dead flower spikes and leaves in autumn. Divide approximately every three or four years if in fairly confined space.

PROPAGATION
By division in spring, by seed in summer, or by removal of root bulbils where these are accessible.

PROBLEMS
Aphids.

Alisma plantago-aquatica

Butomus umbellatus

FLOWERS In summer, fairly large and pink, in attractive spreading umbels.
FOLIAGE Deciduous, narrow, rush-like and twisted, greenish purple with sharp edges.
SITE Full sun to very light shade.
PREFERRED WATER DEPTH 2.5–15cm (1–6in).
RECOMMENDED POOL SIZE Large or medium.
SPECIAL REQUIREMENTS None.
HARDINESS Very hardy, tolerating -20°C (-4°F).
SIZE Will attain 1.25m x 50cm (4ft x 20in) after about two or three years.

RECOMMENDED VARIETIES
Normal species only is available.

MARGINALS

Calla palustris
Bog Arum

❝ *Although there are many water-loving members of the family Araceae, I have always considered this one to be the* real aquatic equivalent to the common woodland lords and ladies, Arum maculatum. *It is seen fairly commonly in the temperate regions of the northern hemisphere, where its rich and glossy, dark green leaves emerge from the mud at pond edges. It has been quite widely naturalized in Britain since the mid-nineteenth century. The small, but typically aroid (arum-type) flower heads are said to be pollinated by water snails and, late in the season, they give rise to rather appealing, bright red fruiting heads.* ❞

PLANTING
As rhizomes in spring, directly into soil in large pools; in baskets in smaller ones.

CARE
Little needed once established but dead foliage should be cut back in autumn and winter.

PROPAGATION
By wholesale division or by simply breaking off pieces of the rhizome in spring; also propagated by seed sown fresh in early autumn directly into wet soil.

PROBLEMS
None.

RECOMMENDED VARIETIES
Normal species only is available.

FLOWERS Tiny, in spring on green and white arum-like spadix borne in a white, rather papery spathe. Fruits, round, bright red on short spikes.
FOLIAGE Deciduous or more or less evergreen, rich, glossy green, broadly heart-shaped with long stalk.
SITE Full sun or very light shade.
PREFERRED WATER DEPTH 5–25cm (2–10in).
RECOMMENDED POOL SIZE Medium or large.
SPECIAL REQUIREMENTS None.
HARDINESS Very hardy, tolerating -20°C (-4°F).
SIZE Will attain 25–30 x 25–30cm (10–12 x 10–12in) after two or three years.

SIMILAR SPECIES
Zantedeschia is similar; see p.58.

Calla palustris

Caltha palustris
Marsh Marigold, Kingcup

❝ *Perhaps the most familiar and most loved native British water-side plant, this is a beautiful water buttercup of imposing proportions, both in its flowers and its leaves. Much of its appeal to me lies in the neatness of its clumps; it never becomes unkempt and straggly in the way of so many true buttercup species.* Caltha *has several interesting flower variants and I am always intrigued by the way that they divide gardeners' opinions. Even Miss Jekyll herself pronounced on her preference for the singles.* ❞

PLANTING
As plants in spring, directly into soil.

CARE
Little needed once established but dead foliage may be cut back and the plants generally tidied up in autumn. In more formal plantings, best divided every four or five years.

PROPAGATION
By division in spring, or by seed sown fresh in early autumn in wet soil.

PROBLEMS
Aphids, mildew.

RECOMMENDED VARIETIES
My strong preference is for the golden-yellow, single flowered normal species but others opt for the highly floriferous and tightly double flowered 'Flore Pleno' or the single white var. *alba*.

Caltha palustris

FLOWERS Golden-yellow, buttercup-like in spring; also occurs in double and white flowered variants.
FOLIAGE Deciduous, more or less rounded, dark green and very glossy, long-stalked.
SITE Prefers full sun or light to medium shade; often found naturally in waterlogged woodland soils.
PREFERRED WATER DEPTH 0–15cm (0–6in).
RECOMMENDED POOL SIZE Preferably medium or large; may be planted as single specimens alongside small pools but doesn't look as effective as in a massed planting.
SPECIAL REQUIREMENTS None.
HARDINESS Very hardy, tolerating -20°C (-4°F).
SIZE Will attain 60 x 50cm (24 x 20in) within three or four years; the double flowered 'Flore Pleno' about half this.

SIMILAR SPECIES
Caltha leptostyla is a smaller, rather dainty North American species with star-like, golden-centred white flowers; much more suitable for smaller pools.

Cotula coronopifolia Brass buttons

❝ At least the name is descriptive, for this tiny aquatic South African daisy does have small, button-like flowers. This is a useful plant for the edges of small, informal pools, partly as it is not very invasive, and because it can't become out of hand as it isn't very long lived, nor very hardy and in cold winters will die, to be renewed again in spring. ❞

PLANTING
As plants in spring, directly into soil.
CARE
None normally needed although, in milder areas where it is truly perennial, it may with advantage be divided every three or four years.
PROPAGATION
By division in spring, or by seed sown in spring in wet soil.
PROBLEMS
None.

RECOMMENDED VARIETIES
The normal species is usually the only form available although a cream-flowered variant, sometimes called 'Cream Buttons', also exists.

FLOWERS Golden-yellow, rounded, button-like for a long period in summer.
FOLIAGE Deciduous, small, narrowly elongated, mid-green, sparsely toothed.
SITE Full sun or very light shade.
PREFERRED WATER DEPTH 0–10cm (0–4in).
RECOMMENDED POOL SIZE Small
SPECIAL REQUIREMENTS None.
HARDINESS Moderately hardy, tolerating -10°C (14°F).
SIZE Will attain about 15 x 30cm (6 x 12in) after two or three years in mild areas.

Cotula coronopifolia

MARGINALS

Equisetum hyemale
Scouring rush

❝ I have been addicted to horsetails ever since my days at primary school when I first learned of the Carboniferous period, for there is something rather special about a plant that has changed little in general form for over two hundred million years. It was ancient relatives of the modern-day species of Equisetum *that populated the coal-forming swamps in the company of primitive reptiles and amphibians. That one of their number is still in the company of the frogs of my garden pool is, therefore, entirely appropriate. Of the numerous extant species, this one,* E. hyemale, *is the best one for a pool. The common name of 'scouring rush' comes from the plant's traditional use as a pot scourer, its silica encrusted tissues working as well as many a present-day abrasive.* ❞

PLANTING
As plants in autumn or spring, directly into soil in large pools; in baskets in smaller ones.

CARE
Little needed, but dead stems may be cut out as necessary (don't pull them as this may result in cut fingers).

PROPAGATION
By division in spring.

PROBLEMS
None.

FLOWERS None, but small greenish 'cones' at tips of stems.
FOLIAGE Evergreen, true leaves tiny and sheath-like around joints of the finely fluted, mainly unbranched green stems.
SITE Full sun to moderate shade.
PREFERRED WATER DEPTH 5-20cm (2-8in).
RECOMMENDED POOL SIZE Small to large.
SPECIAL REQUIREMENTS None.
HARDINESS Hardy to very hardy, tolerating -15 to -20°C (5 to -4°F).
SIZE 1–1.5m x 25cm (3–5ft x 10in) after two or three years.

RECOMMENDED VARIETIES
Normal species only is available.

Equisetum hyemale

Houttuynia cordata

❝ *By and large, I like plants with variegated foliage, but I'm not entirely sure about this one. It has a variety called 'Chameleon', the main reason for its present popularity, that really seems to have just too many colours for its own good. It is an oriental, rather aromatic plant with a peculiar smell, somewhat reminiscent of citrus fruit. Perhaps I am painting too unappetizing a picture, however, for it seems to be the* sine qua non *of modern water gardens; although I still don't have it in mine.* ❞

FLOWERS White, tiny, in early summer, in cone-shaped spikes surrounded by greenish-white bracts.
FOLIAGE Deciduous or more or less evergreen leaves, more or less oval, greenish-blue with reddish margins and red stems.
SITE Light to moderate shade (best planted beneath dappled shade of larger leaved plants).
PREFERRED WATER DEPTH 0–10cm (0–4in).
RECOMMENDED POOL SIZE Small to large.
SPECIAL REQUIREMENTS None.
HARDINESS Hardy to very hardy, tolerating -15 to -20°C (5 to 14°F).
SIZE 30 x 50cm (12 x 20in) after three or four years.

Houttuynia cordata

PLANTING
As plants in autumn or spring, directly into soil in large pools; in baskets in smaller ones.

CARE
Little needed, but foliage may be tidied up in autumn in more formal settings. Divide approximately every three or four years.

PROPAGATION
By division in spring.

PROBLEMS
None.

RECOMMENDED VARIETIES
The normal species with rather bluish-green leaves is infrequently seen, the multi-coloured variety, 'Chameleon' with red, cream, white and green-variegated leaves being much more common. 'Flore Pleno' has double flowers.

Hypericum elodes
Marsh St John's Wort

❝ *Most hypericums are border shrubs of variable merit. This western European species is a creeping herbaceous perennial, also of slightly variable merit, for hypericum flowers are never exciting at the best of times. But for a fairly large planting, where it can make a small contribution to an overall effect, it is probably a plant worth having.* ❞

RECOMMENDED VARIETIES
Normal species only is available.

PLANTING
As plants in autumn or spring, directly into soil in large pools; in baskets in smaller ones.

CARE
Little needed once established but it may be necessary to tidy up the foliage in autumn.

FLOWERS Yellow, small, appearing in summer.
FOLIAGE Deciduous, small, oval pale green leaves on densely white woolly-looking stems.
SITE Full sun to light shade.
PREFERRED WATER DEPTH 0–8cm (0–3in).
RECOMMENDED POOL SIZE Small to medium.
SPECIAL REQUIREMENTS None.
HARDINESS Moderately hardy, tolerating -10 to -20°C (14 to -4°F).
SIZE 20 x 50cm (8 x 20in) after three or four years.

PROPAGATION
By division in spring, or by removal of rooted layers.

PROBLEMS
None.

Hypericum elodes

MARGINALS

Water irises

" It seems likely that the genus Iris *contains species appropriate to a wider range of garden habitats than almost any other. From tiny rock garden bulbs to giant border perennials, there's an iris for almost every situation, the water garden included. While* Iris chrysographes, I. innominata, I. orientalis *and* I. sibirica *are happiest in the bog garden, here I shall concentrate on those that really prefer to have their rhizomes in water:* I. ensata *and* I. laevigata *are Oriental,* I. pseudacorus *is European and* I. versicolor *North American. All have the readily recognizable iris flowers, but I do urge you to be adventurous and not simply accept the varieties that are stocked everywhere – it really will be worth going to a specialist supplier. "*

PLANTING
Ideally as newly sprouting rhizomes in spring although there is also much to be said for buying your plants later when you can see the flower colours. Plant directly into soil in large pools; in baskets in smaller ones.

CARE
Cut back dead flower spikes by cutting at an angle flush with the first sheathing leaf. Cut back old foliage as it discolours in autumn. Divide every three or four years in spring.

PROPAGATION
By division in spring.

PROBLEMS
Aphids, snails.

FLOWERS Familiar and characteristic with three outer parts or falls that hang downwards, and three inner parts or standards, more or less upright. Falls are often marked with contrasting colours. Some species have one flower per stem, others several.

FOLIAGE Deciduous or evergreen, narrow and sword-like with sheathing base.

SITE Full sun to light shade.

PREFERRED WATER DEPTH 2.5–15cm (1–6in), preferably rather less in summer.

RECOMMENDED POOL SIZE Small to large, depending on vigour; *I. pseudacorus* is suitable only for larger pools.

SPECIAL REQUIREMENTS None.

HARDINESS Hardy, tolerating -15°C (5°F); *I. pseudacorus* very hardy, tolerating -20°C (-4°F).

SIZE Varies with species and variety from about 60 x 20cm (2 x 8in) after two years for some of the *I. laevigata* varieties to 2 x 1m (6 x 3ft) for *I. pseudacorus* which does become a very large plant.

RECOMMENDED VARIETIES

Iris ensata (syn. *I. kaempferi*) (reddish-purple), 'Alba' (white), Higo hybrids, (a range including blue, mauve, pink and white, often with flecks and spots), 'Moonlight Waves' (white with greenish centre), 'Rose Queen' (pink), 'Variegata' (purple, leaves striped white). *I. laevigata* (bluish-violet), 'Alba' (white), 'Atropurpurea' (red-purple), 'Colchesterensis' (white with dark blue centre), 'Variegata' (pale blue, leaves striped white), 'Weymouth Midnight' (dark blue with white markings). *I. pseudacorus* (yellow flag iris) (yellow), 'Alba' (white), var. *bastardii* (pale yellow), 'Variegata' (golden-yellow, leaves with golden stripes early in season). *I. versicolor* (red-purple or mauve with darker and white markings), 'Kermesina' (red-purple).

Iris ensata

Iris pseudacorus

Iris laevigata **'Variegata'**

Lobelia cardinalis

❝ *This will come as a surprise to those gardeners used to thinking of lobelias as the mainly blue-flowered, half-hardy, South African summer bedding plants that tumble from hanging baskets and spill over the edges of beds. For this plant is hardier (although not totally tough), aquatic, tall and has red flowers, but a lobelia it certainly is – a North American member of what is a huge genus of over 300 species ranging from tiny annuals to small trees. Lobelia cardinalis is a pool-side gem and in areas where it isn't fully hardy, it should be grown in containers and taken under shelter in the winter.* ❞

PLANTING
As plants in spring, contained in planting baskets.

CARE
Cut back dead flower stems and old foliage in autumn. Lift complete in baskets if necessary, put into larger containers and keep under cover in a greenhouse over winter.

PROPAGATION
By division in spring, also by layering or leaf-bud cuttings in summer.

PROBLEMS
Aphids, fungal leaf spots, snails.

SIMILAR SPECIES
Lobelia fulgens, also from North America, is similar but more graceful. *L. dortmanna* is a more or less submerged rosette-forming species (see p.78).

Lobelia **'Queen Victoria'**

FLOWERS Rich red, in tall spikes, in summer; in form rather like those of a salvia but with very much more class.
FOLIAGE Deciduous, narrowly elongated, reddish-bronze.
SITE Full sun to light shade.
PREFERRED WATER DEPTH 0–10cm (0–4in).
RECOMMENDED POOL SIZE Small to large.
SPECIAL REQUIREMENTS Lift for indoor storage in winter in all except very mild areas.
HARDINESS Fairly hardy, tolerating -5 to -10°C (23–14°F).
SIZE Will attain 1m x 25cm (3ft x 10in) after three years.

RECOMMENDED VARIETIES
The normal species is most frequently seen although there are several rather similar hybrids with *Lobelia cardinalis* as one of the parents. Of these 'Queen Victoria', with blood-red foliage, is particularly fine and fairly easily obtained.

51

MARGINALS

Mentha aquatica
Water mint

> *An abiding memory of student field trips to study the ecology of bogs and marshes is the smell of mint. It came from walking along the edges of pools and ditches and unavoidably trampling* Mentha aquatica *beneath my boots. Like most terrestrial mints, it is a vigorous, invasive plant. In the larger water garden, however, this native European plant is an indispensable component.*

FLOWERS Characteristic of most mints; pale mauve and massed in rather large heads at the ends of the shoots.
FOLIAGE Deciduous, more or less oval, toothed, generally rather woolly-hairy, dark green on green-purple, creeping stems.
SITE Full sun to moderate shade; water mint is among the more shade tolerant aquatic plants and in the wild it scrambles beneath other vegetation.
PREFERRED WATER DEPTH 2.5–15cm (1–6in).
RECOMMENDED POOL SIZE Medium to large.
SPECIAL REQUIREMENTS In all except the largest pools, must be lifted and divided quite frequently.
HARDINESS Very hardy, tolerating -20°C (-4°F).
SIZE Will attain about 1m x 75cm (3ft x 30in) within about two years.

Mentha aquatica

PLANTING
As plants in spring or possibly in autumn. May be planted directly into soil in very large pools but it is so invasive that it is always better in planting baskets.

CARE
Cut back dead stems in autumn and, in all except the largest pools, lift and divide every two or three years to keep within bounds.

PROPAGATION
By division in spring, by stem cuttings in spring or summer, or from seed sown in spring.

PROBLEMS
Mildew, rust (although I find it appearing much less frequently on *M. aquatica* than on some of the herb garden mints).

RECOMMENDED VARIETIES
Normal species only is available.

Menyanthes trifoliata
Bog bean

> *Menyanthes isn't a true, leguminous bean but it does have three-lobed leaves very reminiscent of those of the broad bean, although there the resemblance ends for the flowers and fruits are quite dissimilar. I consider it to be among the more attractive marginals, for the smooth, rather pale green leaves have a graceful simplicity as they emerge from the water at the pool's edge. It is, nonetheless, a somewhat invasive species and is, therefore, a bit of a risk in smaller water gardens. Its rather 'soft' appearance belies a tough character, for this is a very hardy plant indeed from northern temperate regions. I'm told that in some parts of northern Europe an alcoholic drink is prepared from the roots.*

PLANTING
As young plants in spring, most satisfactorily directly into the soil but may be grown in planting baskets in smaller pools.

CARE
Cut back dead shoots in autumn; divide every three or four years.

PROPAGATION
By division in spring.

PROBLEMS
None.

RECOMMENDED VARIETIES
Normal species only is available.

Mimulus Musk

Mimulus flowers are fairly familiar, and are seen growing alongside ditches and pools in North America and also in parts of Europe where they have become naturalized. Of the common species that are most at home in an aquatic habitat (for there are more terrestrial border forms too), one, *Mimulus moschatus*, has an extraordinary history for it was once one of the most richly perfumed of garden flowers but, mysteriously, throughout the world, all strains of the plants lost much of their aroma around the year 1914 and have never recovered it. But, even if you are a *Mimulus* lover, don't plant them in any other than large water gardens for most are fairly invasive and will self-seed.

FLOWERS Small, star-like, pinkish-white in summer in loose heads borne most attractively above the water surface. For this reason, the plant is, I think, better grown in several centimetres of water rather than at the margin itself.
FOLIAGE Deciduous, three-lobed leaves with three smooth, neatly rounded segments.
SITE Full sun.
PREFERRED WATER DEPTH 2.5–25cm (1–10in).
RECOMMENDED POOL SIZE Medium to large.
SPECIAL REQUIREMENTS None.
HARDINESS Very hardy, tolerating -20°C (-4°F).
SIZE Will attain about 75 x 50cm (30 x 20in) after two or three years.

Mimulus luteus

FLOWERS Characteristically two-lipped, rather like snapdragons (*Antirrhinum*), usually yellow, orange or red but sometimes bluish; generally borne in abundance over the plants and sometimes in tall spikes.
FOLIAGE Deciduous, rather small, mid-green, fairly rounded and sometimes toothed leaves on creeping stems.
SITE Full sun to light or more moderate shade.
PREFERRED WATER DEPTH Varies with species, most preferring from 0–7.5cm (0–3in) but a few, including *M. ringens*, prefer a depth of 7.5–15cm (3–6in).
RECOMMENDED POOL SIZE Medium to large.
SPECIAL REQUIREMENTS None.
HARDINESS Very hardy, tolerating -20°C (-4°F).
SIZE Varies with species; most of the more or less creeping forms will attain from 30–45 x 50cm (12–18 x 20in) after three or four years but the more upright *M. lewisii* and *M. ringens* will reach double this height.

PLANTING
As plants in spring, either directly into soil or into planting baskets.
CARE
Cut back dead shoots in autumn; divide every two or three years.
PROPAGATION
By division in spring, by softwood cuttings in summer, or from seed in spring (some forms).
PROBLEMS
Fungal rots, especially *Botrytis* (grey mould).

RECOMMENDED VARIETIES
Mimulus luteus (water musk, yellow musk) yellow flowers with red blotches, from mid- to late summer. *M. ringens* (lavender musk) bluish flowers, summer. *M. moschatus* (monkey musk), yellow flowers, summer. *M. lewisii* (great purple monkey flower), pink to purple-red flowers, summer. A hybrid derived from it, *M. x bartonianus*, is similar.

MARGINALS

Myosotis scorpioides
Water forget-me-not

❝ There are aquatic versions of many plants that we tend to think of purely as normal garden subjects and the forget-me-not is no exception. Indeed, many forget-me-nots revel in hot, dry conditions and many are annual or biennial so it's a surprise to discover this perennial European species that enjoys having its roots in the water. But it is a pleasant surprise for this is unmistakably a real forget-me-not with its cheerful, tiny blue flowers. ❞

Myosotis scorpioides

FLOWERS In summer, small, round, single, bright blue with central eye in contrasting white, pink or yellow.
FOLIAGE Deciduous, small, usually hairy, elongated-oval, bright green leaves on long trailing stems.
SITE Full sun to moderate shade; probably the most shade tolerant of all freely-flowering water plants.
PREFERRED WATER DEPTH 0–10cm (0–4in).
RECOMMENDED POOL SIZE Small to large.
SPECIAL REQUIREMENTS None.
HARDINESS Very hardy, tolerating -20°C (-4°F).
SIZE Will attain about 25 x 60cm (10 x 24in) within two years. The stems are much longer than this but trail and flop.

RECOMMENDED VARIETIES
The normal species is the form seen most often but the selected varieties, 'Mermaid' (particularly large, bright blue flowers that flower for longer) and 'Pinkie' (pink flowers) may also be found.

PROPAGATION
By division in spring, by removal of rooted rhizomes or, with the true species, by removal of any self-sown seedlings.

PROBLEMS
Mildew, aphids.

PLANTING
As plants in spring or possibly in autumn. It is best planted directly into the soil as, although creeping, it is never unduly invasive.

CARE
Cut back dead stems in autumn and, if necessary, lift and divide every two or three years.

Peltandra undulata (syn. *virginica*)
Arrow arum

❝ Yet another member of that invaluable water plant family, the Araceae, peltandras are North American species with especially fine, glossy, arrow-like leaves. They are particularly valuable as members of mixed foliage plantings along the margins of medium to large pools. Because they are individually fairly large and because they do look their best in big groups, however, they really aren't species most suitable for small water gardens. ❞

FLOWERS In late spring, typically aroid, tiny on a short spadix rather closely embraced by the green and white sheathing spathe.
FOLIAGE More or less evergreen, spear- or arrow-shaped, rich glossy green, elongating after the flowers fade. Spike of greenish berries.
SITE Full sun to light shade.
PREFERRED WATER DEPTH 0–25cm (0–10in).
RECOMMENDED POOL SIZE Medium to large.
SPECIAL REQUIREMENTS None.
HARDINESS Hardy, tolerating about -15°C (5°F).
SIZE Will attain about 75 x 45cm (30 x 18in) after two or three years.

Peltandra undulata (syn. virginica)

PLANTING
As plants or rhizomes in spring, preferably directly into the soil; if they need to be confined to baskets, then the pool is probably too small for them.

CARE
Little needed, but dead and dying foliage should be cut back in autumn. In cold areas, it may be advantageous to pack bracken or similar material around the crown for protection in winter where the rhizomes are not covered with water.

PROPAGATION
By division of rhizomes in spring.

PROBLEMS
None.

RECOMMENDED VARIETIES
Normal species only is available.

Ranunculus Spearwort

> *The water-loving buttercup-like plants of the Ranunculaceae seem to be taking progressive steps into the water garden. Caltha palustris (p.46) is really happiest just above the margin, Ranunculus aquatilis is most at home when submerged on a stream bed, while the two European and Asian species of spearwort lie somewhere in between in shallow water. They are unmistakably buttercups, with their cheerful yellow flowers, but as their common name suggests, they have elongated spear-like leaves. I always think they have rather a lot of leaf in relation to the size and number of flowers but they are pretty enough in a mixed planting.*

Ranunculus lingua

FLOWERS In summer, single, yellow, buttercup-like, solitary or in small heads at ends of stems.
FOLIAGE Deciduous, elongated, spear-shaped green leaves.
SITE Full sun to very light shade.
PREFERRED WATER DEPTH 0–10cm (0–4in).
RECOMMENDED POOL SIZE Medium to large, although *R. flammula* is also suitable for small pools.
SPECIAL REQUIREMENTS None.
HARDINESS Very hardy, tolerating -20°C (-4°F).
SIZE *R. lingua* will attain about 1m x 25cm (3ft x 10in) after two or three years; *R. flammula* little more than a third of this.

PLANTING
As plants in spring, preferably directly into the soil but they may also be planted in baskets in smaller pools.

CARE
Cut back dead and dying foliage in autumn. May be divided every three or four years if spreading widely.

PROPAGATION
By division in spring. Also from seed sown in spring.

PROBLEMS
Mildew.

RECOMMENDED VARIETIES
Ranunculus flammula: normal species only is available. *R. lingua*: a variety with showy flowers called 'Grandiflorus' is also seen.

MARGINALS

Sagittaria sagittifolia Arrowhead

❝ This isn't the only arrowhead in the water garden (Peltandra p.54 is another) but, while peltandras are American, the common hardy sagittarias are very much Old World species and one of them, Sagittaria sagittifolia, is one of the more robust and common of native British water-side plants. The leaves are beautiful and well justify their common name but the plant is invasive and should be planted with caution. In larger pools, it tends to be attacked by ducks which eat the tubers; hence the colloquial name 'duck potato'. ❞

Sagittaria sagittifolia

FLOWERS In summer, rather large, white, with a dark purple blotch at the base of the petals.
FOLIAGE Deciduous, with three types of leaf: large, green, glossy and arrowhead-shaped aerial leaves on plants growing as marginals; more or less oval, floating leaves; and elongated, submerged leaves produced when submerged tubers first begin growth in the spring.
SITE Full sun to very light shade.
PREFERRED WATER DEPTH 0–10cm (0–4in) (as marginal) but also up to 60cm (24in) as submerged aquatic.
RECOMMENDED POOL SIZE Medium to large.
SPECIAL REQUIREMENTS None.
HARDINESS Hardy, tolerating -15 to -20°C (5 to 4°F).
SIZE Will attain about 50 x 30cm (20 x 12in) in two years.

PLANTING
As plants or tubers in spring or possibly in autumn. It is best planted directly into the soil by large pools or in large baskets although it really is too vigorous to be properly confined. It may also be grown as a submerged and floating plant by weighting the tubers and dropping them into deeper water.

CARE
Cut back dead stems in autumn and, if necessary, lift and divide every two or three years.

PROPAGATION
By division in spring, by removal and replanting of the overwintering tubers that develop at the tips of the runners in late autumn, or by seed in the spring.

PROBLEMS
Aphids.

RECOMMENDED VARIETIES
The normal species is the form seen most frequently but the double flowered 'Flore Pleno' is particularly attractive. A plant often sold as *S. japonica* is now considered the same species.

Typha Reedmace

❝ The baby Moses was never hidden among a clump of typhas, although you might be forgiven for thinking otherwise as both classical and modern illustrations of the Old Testament story often depict their unmistakable club-like heads and they have, indeed, become popularly known as bulrushes. In reality, the name bulrush is more accurately applied to a species of Scirpus and also to the warm-climate Cyperus papyrus which was probably the plant that provided Moses with his protection. Typha, more usefully and unambiguously called the reedmace, is, however, one of the most stately of temperate water-side genera but almost all are truly invasive and should only be planted beside really large pools. Only T. minima should be considered for planting in smaller water gardens. ❞

PLANTING
As plants in spring or possibly in autumn; best planted directly into the soil by large pools or in large baskets although, with the exception of *T. minima*, they are really too vigorous to be properly confined.

FLOWERS In summer, tiny, in brown, velvety rod or tail-like heads with males above females; in some species the two parts are quite distinct (see Recommended Varieties).
FOLIAGE Deciduous or more or less evergreen, leaves green or grey-green, tough, grass-like, usually embracing the stem and often curiously spongy at the base.
SITE Full sun to very light shade.
PREFERRED WATER DEPTH 0–15cm (0–6in).
RECOMMENDED POOL SIZE Large (except *T. minima*, small or medium).
SPECIAL REQUIREMENTS Take care when planting in pools with butyl or other rubber liners because the tips of the rhizomes, on the larger species especially, are needle-like and will readily cause punctures.
HARDINESS Very hardy, tolerating -20°C (-4°F).
SIZE Varies with species: *T. latifolia* will attain 2.5–3m x 50–75cm (8 x 10ft x 20-30in) after two or three years, *T. angustifolia* two-thirds and *T. laxmannii* one-third of this; *T. mimina* will only reach an approximate height of 45 x 20cm (18 x 8in).

Typha minima

CARE
Cut back dead foliage in autumn. Ideally, the club-like seedheads should also be cut back before they disperse their seeds although, unfortunately, they are the plant's chief attraction.

PROPAGATION
By division in spring, or by removal of the self-sown seedlings.

PROBLEMS
Aphids.

Typha angustifolia

Typha latifolia

RECOMMENDED VARIETIES
Typha latifolia (great reedmace), a huge species with massive, poker-like, flower heads. *T. angustifolia* (lesser reedmace), smaller but still a large plant with club-like heads of female flowers separated by a gap from the tail-like male heads above. *T. laxmannii*, medium-sized with slender female flower heads topped with tail-like male heads. *T. minima*, the smallest species with neat, spherical heads of female flowers topped with a small 'tail'.

MARGINALS

Veronica beccabunga Brooklime

" *I always see this plant in my mind's eye rather as I see* Myosotis scorpioides *for they do, indeed, have much in common. Both have very pretty, small blue flowers, both have a creeping habit and both are water-loving versions of plants that we know more familiarly in terrestrial, even dry habitats. For while the* Myosotis *is a water forget-me-not, this* Veronica *is an aquatic speedwell. In reality,* Veronica *is much the larger genus, embracing around 250 species and V. beccabunga isn't the only aquatic although it is far and away the commonest offered for cultivation. The 'lime' of the common name seems to be derived from an old observed association of the plant with brooks in chalky places.* "

FLOWERS In summer, small, round, single, vivid blue with a tiny white eye although the blue is somewhat variable in intensity.
FOLIAGE Deciduous, small, more or less rounded, rather fleshy green leaves on long creeping stems.
SITE Full sun to moderate shade.
PREFERRED WATER DEPTH 0–10cm (0–4in).
RECOMMENDED POOL SIZE Small to large.
SPECIAL REQUIREMENTS None.
HARDINESS Very hardy, tolerating -20°C (-4°F).
SIZE Will attain about 15 x 45cm (6 x 18in) in two years.

PLANTING
As plants in spring, ideally into planting baskets.
CARE
Little is needed once fully established, although in small pools, dead stems may be trimmed right back in the autumn.
PROPAGATION
By division in spring, by softwood cuttings in summer, by removal of naturally rooted runners, or by seed in spring.
PROBLEMS
Mildew.

RECOMMENDED VARIETIES
Normal species only is available.

Veronica beccabunga

Zantedeschia aethiopica

" *This aroid is sometimes confusingly called the Calla lily, but although it is certainly no lily, it can with justification be considered a warm climate version of Calla. Despite its specific name, it originates in South Africa although it now grows widely throughout warm parts of the world. Its white aroid (arum-like) spathe is probably best known as a cut flower and many variously coloured hybrids have been derived from it specifically for the floristry trade.* "

PLANTING
As rhizomes or young plants in the spring, put directly into soil in very mild areas, otherwise contained within planting baskets or submerged pots.
CARE
In all except mild areas, lift in autumn and pot up for storing with greenhouse or other protection in winter. In mild areas, ensure that crowns are covered by at least 25cm (10in) of water or, alternatively, pack bracken, straw or other protective covering over them.
PROPAGATION
By division or by careful removal of pieces of sprouting rhizome in spring; also by seed in spring.
PROBLEMS
Fungal leaf spot.

SIMILAR SPECIES
Calla is similar; see p.46.

FLOWERS Tiny in spring on a yellow, arum-like spadix borne in a spreading white spathe. Fruits are round, orange on short spikes but not always formed in cooler climates.
FOLIAGE Deciduous or more or less evergreen, rich, glossy green, broadly heart-shaped with long stalk.
SITE Full sun or moderate shade.
PREFERRED WATER DEPTH 5–25cm (2–10in).
RECOMMENDED POOL SIZE Medium or large.
SPECIAL REQUIREMENTS Should be lifted in autumn for winter storage.
HARDINESS Fairly hardy, tolerating -5 to -10°C (23 to 14°F).
SIZE Will attain 30–45 x 25–30cm (12–18 x 10–12in) after two or three years, although may be considerably taller when in the shade of other plants.

Zantedeschia aethiopica 'Green Goddess'

RECOMMENDED VARIETIES

The normal species is the form most frequently seen as a water garden plant although the slightly more vigorous variety, 'Crowborough', is better, having been selected for its greater hardiness. The striking 'Green Goddess' has a green and white spathe and is another outdoor form although slightly more tender, but the many named and coloured hybrids are not really suitable for outdoor pool cultivation in Europe.

Zantedeschia aethiopica 'Crowborough'

WATER PLANTS

Aponogeton distachyos
Water hawthorn, Cape pondweed

" *The name 'Cape pondweed' I can understand for this is a plant that grows in ponds and originates in South Africa. 'Water hawthorn' is more obscure; I can only assume it refers to the sweetly scented flowers. Nonetheless, the fact that* Aponogeton *does have an appealing scent is a very desirable bonus as is the even rarer attribute that in milder areas it will produce its flowers during the winter. A fair degree of shade tolerance adds further to this being one of the very best and most choice of water plants.* "

Aponogeton distachyos

PLANTING
As tubers or plants in spring, ideally into planting baskets.

CARE
Little needed once established although dead foliage should be pulled out if possible in autumn.

FLOWERS In late spring and in autumn, also winter in mild areas; white with dark, almost black anthers, and arranged on a forked stalk. Fruit ripen below water and then float to disperse seeds when they may be collected by net.

FOLIAGE Deciduous in most temperate areas but more or less evergreen in mild places; elongated-oval, mid-green, floating leaves.

SITE Full sun to moderate shade.

PREFERRED WATER DEPTH 25–60cm (10–24in).

RECOMMENDED POOL SIZE Medium to large.

SPECIAL REQUIREMENTS None.

HARDINESS Fairly hardy, tolerating about -5°C (23°F) but safely surviving cold winters in a dormant state in deep water.

SIZE Will attain a spread at water surface of about 1 x 1m (3 x 3ft) after three years.

RECOMMENDED VARIETIES
The normal species only is available although a pinkish-flowered form does exist.

PROPAGATION
By division in spring, or by seed, ideally sown fresh in autumn into submerged pots.

PROBLEM
None.

Hippuris vulgaris
Mare's tail

" *In anticipation of some of the comments that I might receive, no, I'm not suggesting that you plant one of the most ineradicable of weeds in your garden pool. That* is *horsetail,* Equisetum vulgare; *this* is *mare's tail,* Hippuris vulgaris, *although to confuse you even further, there are aquatic species of* Equisetum *and one of them I do, indeed, recommend (p.48). But back to* Hippuris, *which is a native European plant that seems to figure rather infrequently in books on water gardening. This can only be because it is not considered sufficiently meritorious, but I find this a strange conclusion, for its Christmas tree-like form has a special and unusual appeal of which I am very fond. It is tolerant of a wide range of water conditions and may also be grown as a marginal.* "

PLANTING
As plants or rhizomes in spring, ideally into large planting baskets.

CARE
Little needed once established although dead foliage should be pulled out if possible in autumn.

PROPAGATION
By division in spring.

PROBLEMS
None.

RECOMMENDED VARIETIES
Normal species only is available.

FLOWERS In summer, minute, green and insignificant.
FOLIAGE Deciduous, in whorls, short and very narrowly strap-like on the emerged parts of the stem; thinner and more flimsy on submerged portions (and then much more reminiscent of a mare's tail).

SITE Full sun to light shade.
PREFERRED WATER DEPTH 5–60cm (2–24in).
RECOMMENDED POOL SIZE Medium to large.
SPECIAL REQUIREMENTS None.
HARDINESS Very hardy, tolerating -20°C (-4°F).

SIZE Varies with depth of water. When grown as a marginal, will only attain about 30cm (12in) in height, but in deeper water will consistently produce shoots that emerge up to about 30cm (12in) above the surface. Spreads to about 45cm (18in) after two or three years.

Hippuris vulgaris

WATER PLANTS

Nuphar Water lily, Pond lily

❝ *Nuphars are lesser known members of the water-lily family, at least to gardeners, although one of the native European species,* Nuphar lutea, *is much more familiar in the wild. It is a very large, invasive species, with leaves probably bigger than those of any other British plant. It is because of these giant proportions that it should only be planted in the very largest pools and in deep water; in lakes, indeed, rather than in ponds. Apart from its distinctive yellow flowers, the fruits are its most remarkable feature, being markedly flask-shaped and giving rise to one of the common names of 'brandy bottle'. There are, nonetheless, related species with attractive leaf variegations and rather less antisocial dimensions that share a useful degree of shade tolerance.* ❞

FLOWERS In summer, yellow, reddish in some species, bottle-shaped, strongly and rather strangely scented.
FOLIAGE Deciduous, circular or more or less oval, mid-green floating leaves (up to 40 x 30cm (16 x 12in) in *N. lutea*); thin, translucent, feathery, submerged leaves.
SITE Full sun to moderate shade.
PREFERRED WATER DEPTH 1–2.5m (3–8ft) (*N. lutea*); 45–55cm (18–22in) (*N. japonica*); 30–45cm (12–18in) (*N. pumila*).
RECOMMENDED POOL SIZE Medium to large (very large only for *N. lutea*).
SPECIAL REQUIREMENTS Deeper water than most other water plants.
HARDINESS Very hardy, tolerating -20°C (-4°F).
SIZE *N. lutea* will attain a spread at water surface of at least 2 x 2m (6 x 6ft) after two years; the other species barely half this.

RECOMMENDED VARIETIES
Usually, only the normal species of *Nuphar lutea* is available; however, a variegated form is now separated as a distinct species *N. variegata*. The less vigorous *N. japonica* and *N. pumila* are scaled-down versions with few merits over the *Nymphaea* water lilies, but both exist with variegated foliage, a valuable attribute among plants with floating leaves. Both of these forms are not surprisingly called *variegata*.

Nuphar japonica

PLANTING
As rhizomes or young plants in spring; directly into soil in large pools but the smaller species in baskets in smaller ones.

CARE
Little needed although dead foliage should be pulled out, if possible, in autumn when small species are grown in smaller pools.

PROPAGATION
By division in spring.

PROBLEMS
Aphids.

Nuphar lutea

Nymphoides peltata Fringed water lily, floating heart

> *Superficially, very much like a water lily (and also, indeed, a floating heart) but in reality a close relative of the bog bean (p.52), this is a fairly common native plant throughout Europe and Asia and is now rather widely naturalized in North America. Its flowers are pretty enough if you like small yellow blooms, although they don't really stand comparison with real yellow water lilies, either in* Nuphar *or* Nymphaea, *but the leaves are extremely pretty and the combination does make for a very appealing, if invasive, plant for bigger pools.*

FLOWERS In summer, yellow, with tiny fringes or frills to each of the petals.
FOLIAGE Deciduous, circular to heart-shaped, mid-green floating leaves.
SITE Full sun to light shade.
PREFERRED WATER DEPTH 15–45cm (6–18in).
RECOMMENDED POOL SIZE Medium to large.
SPECIAL REQUIREMENTS None.
HARDINESS Very hardy, tolerating -20°C (-4°F).
SIZE Will attain a spread at the water surface of about 60 x 60cm (24 x 24in) after two years.

Nymphoides peltata

PLANTING
As rhizomes or young plants in the spring; preferably contained within planting baskets.

CARE
Pull out dead foliage in the autumn before it sinks and rots.

PROPAGATION
By division in spring.

PROBLEMS
Aphids.

RECOMMENDED VARIETIES
Usually, only the normal species is available although a form called 'Bennettii' is sometimes seen, however this significantly lacks the pretty leaf mottling.

WATER PLANTS

Nymphaea Water lily

The queens of the garden pool by almost anyone's reckoning, water lilies must exist in more flower colours and a greater range of overall vigour than almost any other garden plant. Largely because of the range of colours, which can vary from the most subdued to the most strident, a water lily can affect the overall appearance of your pool to a greater extent than anything else. I have said a water lily, singular rather than plural, quite deliberately because most small pools have room for only one plant. Even in large ones with space for several individuals, you may well share my view that it might be wise to choose all of the same variety because those colours, so numerous and varied, don't always blend well with each other. Indeed, a combination of some of the yellow, red and pink water lilies is as unfortunate a sight as gardening has to offer. And although it is the flowers that first spring to mind when water lilies are discussed, it's worth bearing in mind that some have extremely attractive foliage too.

The wide range of vigour and also of preferred water depth means that the varieties must be selected with considerable care. There are few experiences more frustrating than discovering that, just when your water lily has established itself, the entire water surface of your pool is vanishing beneath its all-covering carpet of foliage.

Nymphaea 'Madame Wilfron Gonnère'

Nymphaea 'Colossea'  *Nymphaea* 'Gonnère'  *Nymphaea* 'Masaniello'

Nymphaea 'Moorei'  *Nymphaea* 'Fabiola'  *Nymphaea alba*

Nymphaea 'Amabilis'  *Nymphaea* 'Marliacea Chromatella'  *Nymphaea* 'Marliacea Rosea'

65

WATER PLANTS

Nymphaea Water lily (continued)

FLOWERS In summer, each lasting for three or four days only before dipping below the water surface, never to return. The plant as a whole continues blooming for several months. The flowers of most hardy, temperate varieties should float on the surface, unlike the tropical forms which carry the blooms on clear stalks. If this tendency to lift the flowers clear of the water does arise in hardy water lilies, it should, in most instances, be taken as an indication that the plant is becoming congested and is ready for division. Each stem bears only one flower and, although they all have the familiar star-like overall shape, there is considerable variation in size, degree of doubling and presence of perfume as well, of course, as colour, which ranges from white through yellow to pinks and reds, although there are no blues and purples in the hardy forms. Some varieties change colour markedly as the flower ages. A few garden varieties set seed but the fruit mature below water and are seldom seen.

FOLIAGE Deciduous, circular or more or less oval, mid-green floating leaves, sometimes with rather attractively indented or wavy margins. Variations include various types of variegation and marbling and differing degrees of red-purple anthocyanin pigmentation; that on the undersides is visible only when a strong wind lifts the leaf briefly from the water's surface revealing the colour.

SITE Must have full sun; nothing less will suffice.
PREFERRED WATER DEPTH Varies with variety (see lists) from about 15cm–1m (6in–3ft).
RECOMMENDED POOL SIZE Small to large, depending on the chosen variety.
SPECIAL REQUIREMENTS Must have a sunny situation and varieties must be chosen with care for pool size and depth. Try to avoid planting where they will be constantly splashed by a fountain.
HARDINESS Very hardy, tolerating -20°C (-4°F).
SIZE Varies widely with variety from about 30 x 30cm (12 x 12in) to 2.5 x 2.5m (8 x 8ft) after three or four years.

Nymphaea 'René Gérard'

PLANTING
As rhizomes or plants in spring; in soil in large pools but directly into baskets in smaller ones.

CARE
Little needed once established although dead foliage should be pulled out in autumn. On large, strong plants, this should be done with a certain amount of care for it is all too easy to tug at an apparently moribund leaf only to find that its stalk is still perfectly strong enough to pull up the whole thing by the roots. Dead flower heads should also be removed fairly quickly before they can become waterlogged and sink. Most varieties will benefit from division in spring approximately every three or four years. See also my general comments on water plant care (p.40).

PROPAGATION
By division in spring.

PROBLEMS
Aphids, water lily beetle, leaf miners, fungal leaf spots, rhizome rots and root rots.

RECOMMENDED VARIETIES

Almost all of the water lilies grown in garden pools are hybrids derived from a number of wild, temperate-climate species. Unfortunately, most garden centres stock only a pitifully small range of varieties and so I do recommend strongly that you visit a specialist water plant supplier before making your selection. Don't be tempted, however, by some of the gloriously coloured tropical water lilies that you see at specialist nurseries, many with remarkable blue flowers. They can only be grown in large pools or tanks of water with a temperature that never falls below 10°C (50°F), something that most gardeners are quite incapable of providing.

Because the considerations of vigour, spread and preferred water depth are at least as important as those of colour, I have incorporated this information here instead of listing it separately, as I have done with other types of water plant. In the following lists, I have marked with an asterisk (*) the most widely available varieties.

LARGE WATER LILIES

For water depth 30cm–1m (12in–3ft). Surface spread up to 1.5m (5ft).

*'Attraction' (rich red with some white streaks, gradually darkening, semi-double, red-brown stamens, green-bronze leaves, magnificent, the best vigorous red); 'Charles de Meurville' (rich red with some white streaks, semi-double, orange-red stamens, deep olive-green leaves with slightly wavy edges); 'Colonel A. J. Welch' (yellow, semi-double, yellow stamens, mid-green, slightly spotted leaves); 'Colossea' (enormous pink flowers, semi-double, yellow stamens, fragrant, green-bronze leaves, markedly hardy and one of the best and most prolific deep-water varieties); 'Gladstoniana' (white, double, fragrant, golden-yellow stamens, dark green leaves, a wonderful plant); 'Gloire du Temple-sur-Lot' (pale pink fading to white, double, yellow stamens, mid-green leaves, shy flowering); 'Mrs Richmond' (pale pink, gradually darkening to red, double, golden-yellow stamens, pale green leaves with slightly wavy edges); *N. alba (the native British and European water lily, white, double, yellow stamens, reddish leaves, gradually becoming mid-green); *N. tuberosa* 'Richardsonii' (white, semi-double, yellow stamens, pale green leaves, rather shy flowering); *N. t.* 'Rosea' (pale pink, double, red stamens, fragrant, pale green leaves with markedly red-striped stalks).

MODERATELY LARGE WATER LILIES

For water depth 20–60cm (8–24in). Surface spread up to 1m (3ft).

'Amabilis' (pale pink, single, yellow stamens, deep red to green, markedly pointed leaves); 'Atropurpurea' (deep red, single to semi-double, red stamens with yellow tips, dark red leaves, turning green); 'Caroliniana Nivea' (white, semi-double, yellow stamens, pale green leaves, very pretty, easy and free-flowering); 'Conqueror' (rich crimson with white flecks, semi-double, yellow stamens, purple leaves, gradually turning green); *'Escarboucle' (crimson, semi-double, fragrant, red stamens with yellow tips, red-green leaves turning green, one of the best and most reliable of all water lilies); 'Gonnère' (white, double, golden-yellow stamens, pale green leaves); 'Madame Wilfon Gonnère' (pink, double, golden stamens, mid-green leaves); *'Marliacea Albida' (white, semi-double, golden stamens, dark green leaves, rich purple beneath); *'Marliacea Carnea' (pale pink, gradually darkening, semi-double, yellow-gold stamens, purple leaves, turning dark green, an easy and free-flowering variety); *'Marliacea Chromatella' (yellow, semi-double, golden stamens, dark green leaves with brown spots, shade tolerant); 'Marliacea Rosea' (mid-pink, semi-double, golden stamens, purple leaves, turning dark green); 'Masaniello' (rose-pink, double, orange stamens, dark green leaves); 'Moorei' (pale yellow, semi-double, yellow stamens, dark green leaves with purplish blotches). *N. odorata* (white, single, golden stamens, purple leaves, turning pale green). 'Odorata William B. Shaw' (rose-pink, semi-double, golden stamens, mid-green leaves); 'René Gerard' (reddish-pink, semi-double, yellow stamens, mid-green leaves, bronze-green beneath); 'Sunrise' (deep yellow, semi-double, fragrant, golden-yellow stamens, green leaves with brownish blotches, wavy margins, reddish beneath); 'William Falconer' (deep red, single to semi-double, red stamens with yellow tips, dark purple-red leaves gradually turning green)

WATER PLANTS

Nymphaea Water lily (continued)

RECOMMENDED VARIETIES (CONTINUED)

SMALL WATER LILIES

For water depth 15–45cm (6–18in). Surface spread up to 60cm (24in).
'Albatross' (white, single, golden stamens, dark red leaves, gradually turning dark green); 'Brackleyi Rosea' (rose-pink, gradually fading, semi-double, fragrant, pink stamens, dark green leaves); 'Commanche' (orange-yellow, slowly turning red, semi-double, orange-red stamens, purple leaves, turning green); 'Firecrest' (pink, semi-double, fragrant, orange stamens with red tips, green-purple leaves); 'Gloriosa' (pale crimson, gradually darkening, semi-double, fragrant, red stamens with gold tips, green-bronze leaves); 'Indiana' (pink, turning orange-red, semi-double, yellow stamens, olive-green leaves with darker mottling); *'James Brydon' (deep red-pink, semi-double to double, fragrant, red stamens with gold tips, dark green to purple leaves with reddish flecks, justifiably one of the most famous and popular of all water lilies); *'Odorata Sulphurea Grandiflora' (yellow, semi-double, yellow stamens, mid-green leaves with brownish marbling, pronounced reddish spots beneath); 'Robinsoniana' (orange-red, semi-double, yellow stamens, dark green leaves with darker flecking); 'Rose Arey' (rose-pink, semi-double, fragrant, orange stamens, purple leaves, gradually turning green, a very good and reliable variety); 'Sioux' (yellow, turning orange then rich red, semi-double, yellow stamens, greenish-bronze leaves with brown mottling and rich brown beneath).

VERY SMALL WATER LILIES

For water depth 10–30cm (4–12in). Surface spread up to 30cm (12in).
'Aurora' (yellow, gradually changing through orange to red, semi-double, yellow stamens, mid-green leaves with mottled and marbled patterns); 'Ellisiana' (pale red, gradually darkening, single, yellow stamens, mid-green leaves); *'Froebelii' (vivid red, single, yellow stamens, mid-green leaves); 'Graziella' (coppery-red, single, orange stamens, pale green leaves with purple flecking). *N. tetragona* (syn. 'Pygmaea Alba') (white, single, golden-yellow stamens, dark green leaves, dark red beneath, very tiny indeed, almost the only water lily that can be grown in an aquarium and now naturalized in Britain); 'Laydekeri Fulgens' (crimson, single, red stamens, dark green leaves with purple-brown flecks); 'Laydekeri Lilacea' (lilac-pink, single, yellow stamens, green leaves with sparse brown flecks); 'Laydekeri Purpurata' (crimson, single, orange stamens, mid-green leaves with purple flecks). *N.* x *helvola* (yellow, single, orange stamens, olive-green leaves). 'Paul Hariot' (yellow, turning reddish-orange, semi-double, fragrant, yellow stamens, mid-green leaves with purplish flecking); 'Solfatare' (yellow, turning orange-yellow and then red, single, yellow stamens, dark green leaves with purple blotches and spots).

Nymphaea 'Froebelii'

Nymphaea x *helvola*

Nymphaea 'James Brydon'

THE AMAZING MONSIEUR MARLIAC

A number of water lily varieties are prefixed by the name 'Marliacea', a reference to the remarkable French plant breeder, Joseph Bory Latour-Marliac, who raised them around the turn of the century. But a very much greater number of varieties (including many of those that I have recommended) also originated in his nursery at Temple-sur-Lot in the south of France. No other single person has contributed as much to the development of the garden water lily, and it is probable that in no other group of plants has one person's influence been so great. The remarkable thing about M. Marliac, and the reason that relatively little has been achieved since, is that we still have scant idea of how he did it. He used a combination of hardy European and American species to produce his hybrids and was mainly responsible for extending the colour range to more than just the chiefly white-flowered varieties available until that time. But the details of his crosses and selections were imparted to no one and he took his carefully guarded secrets with him when he died in 1911.

Nymphaea 'Moorei'

WATER PLANTS

Orontium aquaticum Golden club

❝ Yet another member of the arum family and, I think, my favourite of all water plants in its distinctiveness, for it differs from the more familiar aroids in lacking the sheathing, leafy spathe which is reduced in this plant to form a small basal structure. In consequence, the candle-like flower spike is fully and attractively exposed. Orontium is a one-species North American genus that sells on sight if it is seen in flower although its foliage, too, is attractive and appealing. ❞

FLOWERS In late spring, tiny, on white, cylindrical spikes with pronounced golden tips. Small, green fruits form underwater.
FOLIAGE Deciduous, elongated-oval, dark green, silvery above and purplish beneath, partly aerial, floating or submerged, depending on the depth of the water.
SITE Full sun.
PREFERRED WATER DEPTH 10–45cm (4–18in).
RECOMMENDED POOL SIZE Small to large.
SPECIAL REQUIREMENTS Take care not to disturb when well established.
HARDINESS Moderately hardy to hardy, tolerating about -15°C (5°F).
SIZE Will attain spread at water surface of about 60cm (24in) after two or three years.

Orontium aquaticum

PLANTING
As rhizomes or young plants in spring; preferably into planting baskets first.

CARE
Little needed, but dead foliage should be pulled away in autumn. It is best not disturbed once established.

PROPAGATION
By division in spring, or by seeds sown fresh in submerged pots.

PROBLEMS
None.

RECOMMENDED VARIETIES
Normal species only is available.

Persicaria amphibia (syn. *Polygonum amphibium*)
Amphibious bistort, willow grass

" *This is a curious plant, a member of the large dock family, the Polygonaceae, a group that contains many pestilential and invasive weeds, and is widely spread throughout the temperate northern hemisphere. But notice its name – amphibia, not aquatica – it is a species, therefore, that is at home both on land and in water. In its terrestrial habitat, it can be an invasive weed yet, growing in water, it becomes a more docile creature, much less prone to get out of hand and can, indeed, be most attractive. I'm surprised more water plant nurseries don't stock it.* "

FLOWERS In late summer, tiny, neat pink or reddish spikes.
FOLIAGE Deciduous, elongated-oval, mid-green, mostly floating but aerial in shallow water.
SITE Full sun to light shade.
PREFERRED WATER DEPTH Best in 30–45cm (12–18in); in shallower water it becomes invasive.

PLANTING
As young plants in spring; either directly in soil in large pools or, perhaps better, into planting baskets.

CARE
Little needed, but dead foliage may be cut away in autumn if the plant is in fairly shallow water.

RECOMMENDED POOL SIZE Medium to large.
SPECIAL REQUIREMENTS Try to restrict to deeper water.
HARDINESS Very hardy, tolerating -20°C (-4°F).
SIZE Will attain spread at water surface of about 60cm (24in) after two or three years.

RECOMMENDED VARIETIES
Normal species only is available.

PROPAGATION
By division in spring or by seeds sown fresh in damp soil.

PROBLEMS
Aphids, fungal leaf spots.

Persicaria amphibia

WATER PLANTS

Pontederia cordata Pickerel weed

"I wondered for many years what a pickerel was. Being an angler I really should have known, for it is a local name for various species of pike which, apparently, hide among this plant at the water's edge in its native North American home. The various forms are often listed as marginals but, rather like Persicaria amphibia *(p.71) and* Sparganium *(p.73), they can become invasive and troublesome when grown in this way and I prefer to treat them as deeper water aquatics. I assume and hope that your garden pool doesn't contain pike but, if it is large enough, this is a fine plant to grow for there are very few blue-flowered aquatics, and even fewer that bloom in late summer."*

FLOWERS In summer until early autumn, tiny, massed in spikes, very pale blue.
FOLIAGE Deciduous, often more or less spear-shaped, glaucous leaves emerging from water.
SITE Full sun.
PREFERRED WATER DEPTH 10–30cm (4–12in) but best and most manageable in a depth of 25–30cm (10–12in).

RECOMMENDED POOL SIZE Medium to large.
SPECIAL REQUIREMENTS Try to avoid planting in shallow water where it will soon become a nuisance.
HARDINESS Very hardy, tolerating -20°C (-4°F).
SIZE Will attain spread at water surface of about 45–50cm (18–20in) after two years.

RECOMMENDED VARIETIES
There is a form, *alba*, with white flowers which seems rather to miss the point of the plant; also a variety *lancifolia* with more narrowly elongated leaves and usually darker blue flowers. A plant sometimes listed as *Pontederia azurea* is now more correctly called *Eichornia crassipes* (p.82).

PLANTING
As young plants in spring; directly into the soil in very large pools but otherwise into planting baskets.

CARE
Little care is needed once the plants are fully established, but any dead foliage should be pulled away as autumn approaches.

PROPAGATION
By division of the plants in the spring, or by seeds sown fresh into submerged pots.

PROBLEMS
None.

Pontederia cordata

Sparganium erectum Burr reed

"*Not a reed, although certainly well equipped with burrs, this is another of those plants that behaves itself better when it is moved from the pool edge into deeper water. It's a common enough British water-side species, but you don't need to be familiar with it in its native habitat for long before its aggressive nature becomes evident. If you have a small pool, avoid it; if you have a larger one, plant it in deeper water and admire the sharply branched flowering spikes with the small, spherical, prickly flower and fruiting heads that give the species its common name.*"

FLOWERS In summer, small, green, massed in globose, spiky heads; the female flowers are larger and positioned towards the bases of the branched stalks.
FOLIAGE Deciduous or more or less evergreen in milder areas, long, green, rather iris-like leaves.
SITE Full sun to more moderate shade.
PREFERRED WATER DEPTH 10–30cm (4–12in) but best and most manageable in 25–30cm (10–12in).
RECOMMENDED POOL SIZE Medium to large.
SPECIAL REQUIREMENTS Try to avoid planting in shallow water where it will soon become a nuisance.
HARDINESS Very hardy, tolerating -20°C (-4°F).
SIZE Will attain about 1–1.5m x 60cm (3–5ft x 24in) (depending on water depth) after two or three years.

Sparganium erectum

PLANTING
As young plants in spring; directly into the soil in very large pools but otherwise into planting baskets.

CARE
Little needed, but dead stems and foliage should be cut away in autumn.

PROPAGATION
The easiest methods to use are either by division of the plants in spring, or by seeds sown fresh in submerged pots.

PROBLEMS
None.

RECOMMENDED VARIETIES
Normal species only is available.

SUBMERGED PLANTS

Callitriche Water starwort

❝ Among the more functional, rather than beautiful, oxygenating plants, the various species of Callitriche are widespread in their natural distribution throughout Europe and North America but much less common in aquatic plant nurseries. This is rather a pity because it is a plant especially attractive to fish for laying their spawn and it also provides a habitat for minute pond life on which the young fish will feed. ❞

RECOMMENDED VARIETIES
Callitriche hermaphroditica (syn. *autumnalis*) is the most frequently seen and best species. *C. palustris* (also known as *C. verna*) dies down in winter.

PLANTING
As young plants in spring; in planting baskets in large pools or as weighted clumps sunk into smaller ones.

CARE
None normally needed although this is a fairly fast-growing species and will need thinning out every two years.

FLOWERS Insignificant.
FOLIAGE Evergreen, tiny, narrowly elongated and arising in opposite pairs, mid-green, forming rather pretty floating rosettes at the water surface; also some aerial, spear-shaped leaves.
SITE Full sun to very light shade.
PREFERRED WATER DEPTH 10–50cm (4–20in).
RECOMMENDED POOL SIZE Small to large.
SPECIAL REQUIREMENTS None.
HARDINESS Very hardy, tolerating -20°C (-4°F).
SPREAD Indefinite.

PROPAGATION
By division in spring or by cuttings, weighted and dropped straight into the water.

PROBLEMS
None.

Callitriche palustris

Ceratophyllum demersum Hornwort

❝ This is, perhaps, the best oxygenating plant for milder areas with warmer water and, in consequence, slightly less reliable in colder regions. Like many submerged plants, it has an almost worldwide distribution. The common name comes from the spiny edges to the leaves. It is a vigorous plant, and in hot summers, can rapidly choke a small pool entirely with a huge mass of dense, floating vegetation that is very attractive to fish and other pond life but also attractive to blanket weed which will readily grow on, over and through it. It never seems to produce roots and floats both at the surface and in mid-water. ❞

FLOWERS Insignificant.
FOLIAGE Evergreen in mild areas, but semi-evergreen in colder ones, the plant sinking to the pool bed; tiny, needle-like, green leaves in whorls.
SITE Full sun.
PREFERRED WATER DEPTH 25cm–1.5m (10in–5ft).
RECOMMENDED POOL SIZE Medium to large.
SPECIAL REQUIREMENTS None.
HARDINESS Hardy, tolerating -10 to -15°C (14–5°F).
SPREAD Indefinite.

RECOMMENDED VARIETIES
Normal species only is available.

PLANTING
As young plants in spring; simply toss them into the water.

CARE
Must be thinned out at least once a year in all except the largest pools.

PROPAGATION
By breaking off small pieces and dropping them into the water; I can't think of any other plant propagation that is easier.

PROBLEMS
None.

Ceratophyllum demersum

Crassula helmsii

Crassula helmsii (syn. Tillaea recurva)

> *There's no doubt that some odd things grow on the bottom of ponds and* Crassula helmsii *proves the point, as it is almost an aquatic succulent. Yes, it is a real* Crassula, *a native of New Zealand and Australia but widely naturalized in Europe, that creeps along the floor of the pool where no one notices it, happily oxygenating away, until some of the stems reach the water surface. It is a moderately good oxygenator but is invasive and, as it lacks any honest good looks, it only really merits a place in large pools.*

PLANTING
As young plants in spring, weighted individually and then dropped into the water.

CARE
Should be thinned out every two or three years in all except the largest pools but this is difficult because of

Crassula helmsii

its inaccessibility – another reason for confining it to large pools.

PROPAGATION
Ideally by division in spring but more easily by taking cuttings, weighting them and dropping them straight into the water.

FLOWERS In summer, more or less insignificant, white, growing near the tops of the stems.
FOLIAGE Evergreen, leaves tiny, needle-like and densely packed together on the long, branching stems which are commonly seen floating at the water's surface.
SITE Full sun.
PREFERRED WATER DEPTH 25cm–1m (10in–3ft).
RECOMMENDED POOL SIZE Medium to large.
SPECIAL REQUIREMENTS None.
HARDINESS Fairly hardy, tolerating around -10°C (14°F) but readily surviving cold winters in deep water.
SPREAD Indefinite.

PROBLEMS
None.

RECOMMENDED VARIETIES
Normal species only is available.

SUBMERGED PLANTS

Eleocharis acicularis Spike rush

" Yet again, the ability of nature to mystify and entrance us is manifest in the garden pool because this, for once, is a true rush, a member of the family Cyperaceae, but unlike its fellow rushes it is as a submerged oxygenating aquatic that it is best used in the water garden. Eleocharis acicularis is a common and widespread species throughout both Europe and North America and in the wild it is equally happy when found growing in the mud at the water's edge. "

Eleocharis acicularis

gradually spreads by runners to form an underwater 'lawn', which should be thinned out every few years. Be warned that this is not a task that is easily done while remaining dry.

PROPAGATION
By division in spring.

PROBLEMS
None.

RECOMMENDED VARIETIES
Normal species only is available.

FLOWERS Only usually formed on plants growing in mud.
FOLIAGE Evergreen, wiry, green-brown, tufted leaves.
SITE Full sun to light shade.
PREFERRED WATER DEPTH Ideally 10-30cm (4-12in) when grown submerged.
RECOMMENDED POOL SIZE Small to large.
SPECIAL REQUIREMENTS None.
HARDINESS Very hardy, tolerating -20°C (-4°F).
SPREAD Height up to about 30cm (12in), depending on water depth; spread on pool floor to about 60cm (24in) in three years.

PLANTING
As young plants in spring; most readily by dropping them individually weighted into the water.

CARE
None normally needed although it

Elodea canadensis Canadian pondweed

" The Canadian pondweed is one of the most mischievous of all pond plants. Not surprisingly, it originated in North America but it was introduced to Europe in the early nineteenth century and very soon blocked rivers, and, at the time, even more importantly, the much-used canals, causing severe obstruction to essential boat traffic. Eventually, the thing quietened down and it is now thought that the original introduction was of a vigorous male clone; the type now sold for water garden use is female and much better behaved. However, it will still need some tending and it is not a plant which should be left to its own devices for long periods. "

RECOMMENDED VARIETIES
Normal species only is available.

SIMILAR SPECIES
The related species, *Elodea callitrichoides* and *E. nuttallii*, require warmer conditions and are better as aquarium plants. Two other common and related species are *E. densa* (now called *Egeria densa*) and *E. crispa* (now called *Lagarosiphon major*) with rather curly leaves which may be grown in pools but, in my experience, they too are much better grown in aquaria.

Elodea canadensis

FLOWERS Sparse, tiny, purple-green at water surface in the summer.
FOLIAGE Deciduous, elongated, fragile bright green leaves in whorls on very long branching stems.
SITE Full sun to light shade.
PREFERRED WATER DEPTH Ideally 10cm–1m (4in–3ft).
RECOMMENDED POOL SIZE Medium to large.
SPECIAL REQUIREMENTS None.
HARDINESS Moderately hardy, tolerating about -5°C (23°F) but surviving cold winters as dormant winter buds.
SPREAD Individual stems reach about 3m (10ft) but the plant forms a large, tangled mass up to 1 × 1m (3 × 3ft) within a year.

PLANTING
As young plants in spring; most readily by dropping them individually weighted into the water.

CARE
Pull it out by the armful every season to avoid it taking over even the largest pool completely.

PROPAGATION
By pulling off pieces in spring, weighting them and dropping them into the water. The plant survives naturally over winter by producing special survival buds that drop into the mud in the autumn.

PROBLEMS
None, although it does seem to me to have a particularly tiresome propensity for attracting blanket weed growth (see p.43).

Fontinalis antipyretica Water moss, Willow moss

❝ *I'm sure this must be the only species of moss that gardeners can buy to grow in their gardens, even if it is to be planted underwater. Fontinalis is a true moss with a widespread natural distribution in temperate climates. It is a pretty little thing, forming dark green, feathery tufts that anchor on to submerged stones and sway characteristically in the current of natural streams. I feel it is much better suited to flowing than still water but will, nonetheless, succeed in fairly shallow, clear pools where fish seem to take particular pleasure in spawning in it.* ❞

PLANTING
As young plants in spring; ideally, these should be bought already attached to small stones which are ready for dropping in the water but, failing this, the stones may be tied in place with plastic thread.

CARE
None necessary.

PROPAGATION
By breaking up large clumps, ideally with a piece of stone attached.

PROBLEMS
None.

RECOMMENDED VARIETIES
Normal species only is available.

FLOWERS None.
FOLIAGE Evergreen, broadly-elongated, dark green leaves in three rows wrapped tightly along very thin branched stems.
SITE Full sun to more moderate shade.
PREFERRED WATER DEPTH Up to 60cm (24in).
RECOMMENDED POOL SIZE Small to large.
SPECIAL REQUIREMENTS None.
HARDINESS Very hardy, tolerating -20°C (-4°F).
SPREAD Individual stems may reach up to 75cm (30in) but are generally shorter, especially in still water; clumps spread to about 15cm (6in) at the base in three years but the plant splays out from this.

Fontinalis antipyretica

SUBMERGED PLANTS

Lobelia dortmanna Water lobelia

❝Lobelia *is a strange genus, and no mistake. Those gardeners used to seeing tender lobelias in hanging baskets will already have been amazed, and I hope entranced, by the almost hardy, rich red-flowered marginal,* Lobelia cardinalis *(p.51); but now we have a genuinely hardy submerged plant in this species from North America and parts of Europe, including Britain. Seen out of flower, it does look purely functional, its hollow stems all but lacking foliage; but when the little nodding pale lilac flowers peep above the water surface in bell-shaped pendants, it combines a certain beauty with its basic oxygenating role.*❞

> **FLOWERS** In summer, pendent, bell-shaped, pale lilac, in small inflorescences above the surface of the water.
> **FOLIAGE** Evergreen, elongated dark green leaves in a rosette, from which the almost leafless stems arise.
> **SITE** Full sun to light shade.
> **PREFERRED WATER DEPTH** Ideally 10–60cm (4–24in).
> **RECOMMENDED POOL SIZE** Small to large.
> **SPECIAL REQUIREMENTS** None, although always best in slightly acidic water.
> **HARDINESS** Very hardy, tolerating -20°C (-4°F).
> **SPREAD** Stems extend to about 60cm (24in); spread on pool floor reaches about 30cm (12in) in three years.

PLANTING
As young plants in spring, most readily by dropping them, individually weighted, into the water.

CARE
None needed.

Lobelia dortmanna

PROPAGATION
By division in spring.

PROBLEMS
None.

> **RECOMMENDED VARIETIES**
> Normal species only is available.

Myriophyllum Water milfoil

❝*Although it may be hard to be over-enthusiastic about any plant that spends its life almost wholly submerged, I think that I would opt for the myriophyllums as my favourite and the most beautiful oxygenators.* Myriophyllum *is a fairly large genus of worldwide distribution and includes some tender species suitable for heated aquaria as well as hardy outdoor aquatics. Its name says it all —* Myriophyllum, *many leaved — although, perhaps rather more accurately, it should be described as 'numerous leaves, greatly divided'.*❞

> **RECOMMENDED VARIETIES**
> *Myriophyllum verticillatum*, leaves usually in whorls of five, finely subdivided. *M. spicatum*, leaves usually in whorls of four, more coarsely subdivided.
> *M. aquaticum*, leaves in whorls of four or five, subdivided but with very short segments.

PLANTING
As young plants in spring; most readily by dropping them, individually, weighted into the water.

CARE
None needed.

PROPAGATION
By cuttings pulled off in the spring and rooted by weighting them into submerged mud.

PROBLEMS
None.

Myriophyllum verticillatum

FLOWERS In summer, minute, pink or yellowish, appearing on long spikes protruding above the water's surface.
FOLIAGE Evergreen, in regular whorls along the stem, usually finely divided to give an overall feathery appearance; where leaves appear on stems above the water surface, they are generally much less divided than those below.
SITE Full sun to light shade.
PREFERRED WATER DEPTH Ideally 10–60cm (4–24in).
RECOMMENDED POOL SIZE Small to large.

SPECIAL REQUIREMENTS None, although *M. verticillatum* and *M. spicatum* are always best in alkaline water.
HARDINESS Very hardy (*M. verticillatum* and *M. spicatum*) tolerating -20°C (-4°F); fairly hardy (*M. aquaticum*) tolerating about -5°C (23°F) but generally surviving colder weather by dying down to a crown in deep water.
SPREAD Varies with species but stems extend to 2–3m (6–10ft); spread on pool floor reaches about 30cm (12in) in three years, and the plant splays out from this.

Myriophyllum aquaticum

SUBMERGED PLANTS

Potamogeton Pondweed

" To a botanist, Potamogeton, the unenterprisingly named pondweed, is a nightmare of a genus. This is due mainly to the fact that its numerous species vary so greatly under different environmental conditions, that it becomes almost impossible to decide where one ends and another begins. To the water gardener, the species can be limited to two main types, neither very exciting, but functional if given space. They generally die down to overwintering buds. From these new growth arises afresh each spring. Potamogeton is a plant for the large pool or lake rather than the small domestic water garden. "

FLOWERS In summer, small, in greenish-brown spikes emerging above the water.
FOLIAGE Deciduous, entirely submerged, dark green leaves, elongated, strap-like with wavy edges and reminiscent of seaweed in *P. crispus*; narrow and grass-like in *P. pectinatus*.
SITE Full sun to light shade.
PREFERRED WATER DEPTH 10–60cm (4–24in).

PLANTING
As young plants in spring.
CARE
Even in large pools, they will require thinning out annually.
PROPAGATION
By division in spring.

RECOMMENDED POOL SIZE Large.
SPECIAL REQUIREMENTS None.
HARDINESS Very hardy, tolerating -20°C (-4°F).
SPREAD Stems extend to 1–2m (3–6ft); spreading over the pool floor these stems reach about 30cm (12in) in three years and the plant growth then emanates out from this.

PROBLEMS
None.

RECOMMENDED VARIETIES
Potamogeton crispus, wavy leaves.
P. pectinatus, finely divided, rather grass-like leaves.

Potamogeton pectinatus

Ranunculus aquatilis

Ranunculus aquatilis
Water crowfoot

> *Several close relatives of the buttercup grace various parts of the water garden but only one, this one, is almost entirely submerged, although I'm never really sure how effective it is as an oxygenator. Like* Potamogeton*, it presents botanists with taxonomic difficulties but is a very much more attractive plant and, given space, its beautiful white buttercup flowers will sit in great profusion on the water's surface.*

PLANTING
As young plants in spring.

CARE
Even in very large pools, it will almost certainly require periodic thinning out if it is not to choke the water completely.

FLOWERS In summer, buttercup-like but pure white with golden centres, floating above the water on short stalks.
FOLIAGE Deciduous, dark green, more or less circular, floating leaves and also very finely divided, grass-like submerged leaves.
SITE Full sun to moderate shade.
PREFERRED WATER DEPTH
10–60cm (4–24in).

PROPAGATION
By division in spring.

PROBLEMS
None.

RECOMMENDED VARIETIES
Normal species only is available.

RECOMMENDED POOL SIZE
Large.
SPECIAL REQUIREMENTS
None.
HARDINESS Very hardy, tolerating -20°C (-4°F).
SPREAD Stems extend to 1.5m (5ft); they spread on the pool floor to about 30cm (12in) in three years, and the plant then splays out from this.

FLOATING PLANTS

Azolla caroliniana Fairy moss

❝On p.77, I described Fontinalis, *a plant that I referred to as, probably, the only moss to be grown deliberately as a garden subject. This being the case, where does that leave this delightful, fairy-like item of vegetation? As yet another water garden misnomer, but also as yet another of water gardening's curiosities for while it is no moss, it is no flowering plant either, but the only floating fern in cultivation. Although* Azolla caroliniana *is a native of the warm parts of North America, it survives the British winters very happily because of the small dormant buds that lie in the basal mud.*❞

FLOWERS None.
FOLIAGE Deciduous, tiny, knobbly green fronds turning rich red in autumn.
SITE Full sun to very light shade.
RECOMMENDED POOL SIZE Small, so that it can be contained by netting. In large pools it will rapidly become out of hand and a nuisance.
SPECIAL REQUIREMENTS Unreliable in moving water.
HARDINESS Barely hardy, tolerating -5°C (23°F) but surviving much colder winters in a dormant state.
SPREAD Will cover about 1sq m (3sq ft) after one year.

RECOMMENDED VARIETIES
Normal species only is available although a few related less hardy species are sometimes offered for aquarium use. *Azolla filiculoides* is sometimes sold for outdoor use but, in my experience, it is less likely to survive cold winters.

PLANTING
As a few fronds, dropped directly into the water.
CARE
Net regularly to limit spread.
PROPAGATION
By simple removal of fronds.
PROBLEMS
None.

Azolla caroliniana

Eichornia crassipes Water hyacinth

❝Eichornia *is a real Jekyll and Hyde plant. In its native South American habitat and also in warm, temperate parts of the world, it can be a terrible nuisance as it multiplies to the extent of severely blocking rivers and other waterways. Indeed, in North America, there are even strict restrictions on its sale for garden use but, in other countries, in small pools in colder areas, where winter temperatures will limit its ambitions, it is a most attractive and valuable floating plant. Its long dangling roots provide fish with convenient spawning places and protection for their young. Its common name is rather appropriate, for the very pretty flowers do indeed closely resemble hyacinth blooms.*❞

PLANTING
As two or three individual plants, dropped into the water in spring.
CARE
Thin out plants during the summer whenever they threaten to cover the pool. In autumn, pot up a few plants in moist compost in a cool greenhouse ready to replenish the stock in the pool the following spring.
PROPAGATION
By removal of the young plants on runners at the water's surface.
PROBLEMS
None.

FLOWERS In summer, bluish-violet, arising above water surface rather like lax hyacinths or even irises.
FOLIAGE Deciduous, curious and appealing, bright green, thick, fleshy leaves with greatly inflated stalks that form floating bladders.
SITE Full sun.
RECOMMENDED POOL SIZE Small to large.
SPECIAL REQUIREMENTS A greenhouse to provide protection for overwintered plants.
HARDINESS Barely hardy, tolerating 0 to -5°C (32–23°F) but stock plants are easily kept over winter.
SPREAD Will cover about 1sq m (3sq ft) within a year.

RECOMMENDED VARIETIES
Normal species only is generally available although sometimes larger flowered and also pink- and yellowish-flowered selections are offered.

Hottonia palustris Water violet

> *Not surprisingly, not a violet; but surprisingly, a member of the primula family. And, perhaps, surprisingly too, a native British plant albeit a rather rare one. It isn't a complete floater, for in shallow water, it will root in the basal mud but, as a pool plant, it is at its best in slightly deeper conditions where it will linger just below the surface for the early part of the summer, and then thrust up a mass of spikes of pale lavender flowers. Look closely (without falling in the water) and you will see why* Hottonia *is a member of the Primulaceae.*

PLANTING
As individual plants, dropped into the water in spring.

CARE
Thin out plants during the summer if they threaten to cover the pool. In the autumn, it dies down to survive as dormant buds.

PROPAGATION
By removal of young plants or by rooting in wet mud in summer.

PROBLEMS
None.

FLOWERS In summer, pale lilac or almost white, in spikes above the water's surface, superficially like those of lady's smock (*Cardamine*).
FOLIAGE Deciduous, in whorls or alternate, mid-green, finely divided and feathery.
SITE Full sun to light shade.
RECOMMENDED POOL SIZE Small to large.
SPECIAL REQUIREMENTS None.
HARDINESS Very hardy, tolerating -20°C (-4°F).
SPREAD Will cover about 1sq m (3sq ft) within a year.

RECOMMENDED VARIETIES
Normal species only is available.

Eichornia crassipes

Hottonia palustris

FLOATING PLANTS

Hydrocharis morsus-ranae Frogbit

" At first sight, the frogbit looks very similar to a baby water lily but closer inspection will also reveal that it is floating rather than rooted, and one can clearly observe that its flowers characteristically have only three petals. It is a native plant of Europe, including Britain, where, if not kept in tight check, it can quickly block up small stagnant pools. However, having said this, it is a pretty thing both in its flowers and foliage and it would be a great shame to exclude it from a garden pool simply because it will need watching and an occasional thinning out before it can become invasive. "

FLOWERS In summer, white with yellow centres, three-petalled, rising above the water's surface.
FOLIAGE Deciduous, rounded or kidney-shaped, green-bronze leaves, both floating and raised above the water surface.
SITE Full sun to very light shade.
RECOMMENDED POOL SIZE Small to large.
SPECIAL REQUIREMENTS Always best grown in still, alkaline water.
HARDINESS Very hardy, tolerating -20°C (-4°F) and surviving the winter as dormant buds.
SPREAD Will cover about 1sq m (3sq ft) after one year.

Hydrocharis morsus-ranae

RECOMMENDED VARIETIES
Normal species only is available.

PLANTING
As young plants in spring, simply dropped into the water.

CARE
Thin out the plants occasionally with a net to limit the spread, otherwise blockage of small pools may occur.

PROPAGATION
By careful removal of the young plantlets that form on runners. Produces terminal buds in winter.

PROBLEMS
Snails.

Lemna Duckweed

" *Duckweed is one of those plants for which I have always had a soft spot. As a child, perhaps it was because of the pleasure I gained from seeing frogs poking their heads through its light green, all-embracing carpet. Since, I have admired it botanically as one of the smallest of all flowering plants, with each tiny frond or thallus being a complete individual. But although duckweeds do sometimes produce flowers, their main method of reproduction is by vegetative division which they achieve with remarkable rapidity, and I must confess that I am more often asked how to remove duckweed from a pool than how to establish it. And the answer is that I don't think it can be removed; so be warned and, if you don't want it, it's worth checking other water plants carefully for the presence of contaminating duckweed before introducing them to the pool. In a large pool, however, it is worth bearing in mind that the name, duckweed, does come from the fondness that ducks and other waterfowl have for the plant as their food.* "

FLOWERS In summer, flowers uncommon and minute.
FOLIAGE Deciduous, variously shaped, individual minute fronds, each usually producing a single dangling root.
SITE Full sun to light or almost moderate shade.
RECOMMENDED POOL SIZE Small to large.
SPECIAL REQUIREMENTS None, but always best in still or almost still water.
HARDINESS Very hardy, tolerating -20°C (-4°F) and surviving the winter as dormant buds.
SPREAD Will cover about 1 sq m (3 sq ft) after the first year, but very rapidly covers even large pools thereafter.

RECOMMENDED VARIETIES
Four species are commonly seen, differing in the shape of their fronds: *Lemna minor* (common duckweed) is rounded; *L. trisulca* (ivy-leaved duckweed), is elongated-oval at right angles, forming a star-shape that usually floats just below the surface; *L. gibba*, rounded, swollen; *L. polyrhiza*, rounded with a tuft of roots. The related *Wolffia arrhiza* is the smallest European flowering plant, rootless and little more than a floating blob of green tissue – hardly the most beautiful thing you've ever seen, but certainly an unusual plant.

PLANTING
As several small plants dropped into the pool in spring.
CARE
Use a net to thin out plants regularly to prevent rapid spreads.
PROPAGATION
By removal of a few fronds.
PROBLEMS
None.

Lemna gibba

FLOATING PLANTS

Stratiotes aloides Water soldier

❝ It will be evident from the entries in this book that the common names of many water plants are, at best, fanciful and, at worst, botanically downright misleading. This one comes into the very fanciful category, for the narrowly pointed leaves are supposed to resemble swords; hence water soldier. In reality, I'm always surprised that it has never been called the water pineapple, as it looks more like a floating pineapple top than anything. In common with one or two other invasive species, its sale is restricted in the United States and other warm areas but it is widely distributed in Europe, including Britain and has a curious habit of rising and sinking in the pool like a yo-yo. It floats just below the surface until mid-summer, then rises, flowers, sinks to the pool bottom and produces peculiar large buds. It then rises to the surface again, the buds develop into young plants, separate from the parent plant and then they sink to the bottom until the spring when, yes, you've guessed it, they rise again to the surface. ❞

FLOWERS In summer, small, white and usually rather hidden among the foliage.
FOLIAGE More or less evergreen with a stiff rosette of toothed, rather narrowly elongated leaves.
SITE Full sun to light shade.
RECOMMENDED POOL SIZE Small to large.
SPECIAL REQUIREMENTS Always prefers still, alkaline water and is best cultivated in water at least 30cm (12in) deep to allow the plants to sink out of harm's way.
HARDINESS Very hardy, tolerating -20°C (-4°F).
SPREAD Will cover about 1 sq m (3 sq ft) after one year.

RECOMMENDED VARIETIES
Normal species only is available.

PLANTING
As young plants in spring, dropped into the water.
CARE
Thin out plants occasionally with a net to limit spread.
PROPAGATION
By removal of the young plants that develop in spring.
PROBLEMS
None.

Stratiotes aloides

Trapa natans Water chestnut

❝ Yes, this is the water chestnut found so commonly in Chinese restaurants. The large thorny fruit is the edible part of the plant, but don't be tempted to nibble any that may be growing in your pool as *Trapa natans* is poisonous when raw. In reality, it is strictly a rooted aquatic but the leaf rosettes, which arise on long stems, appear to be floating free. It is yet another plant that has restrictions placed on its sale in warm countries, for it can cause severe blockages in waterways but in Britain this is unlikely to become a problem because of the cooler climate. The plant is certainly unlike much else in the pool, with its rosettes of peculiar leaves and their very unusual inflated stalks. ❞

PLANTING
As young plants in spring, dropped into the water or as fruits (see under propagation, p.41).
CARE
Thin out plants occasionally in order to limit spread.
PROPAGATION
By the large spiny fruits which will germinate in the pool mud in spring and give rise to a stem from which the floating leaves develop.
PROBLEMS
None.

RECOMMENDED VARIETIES
Normal species only is available.

Trapa natans

FLOWERS In summer, small, white and well hidden among the foliage.
FOLIAGE Deciduous, annual, with a floating rosette of rather angular, toothed leaves, each on an inflated stalk.
SITE Full sun to light shade.
RECOMMENDED POOL SIZE Small to large.
SPECIAL REQUIREMENTS Always best in almost still, slightly acidic water, preferably at least 30cm (12in) deep. See also comments under hardiness (below).
HARDINESS Barely hardy, tolerating about -5°C (23°F) and although it will survive winters as the fruits in a dormant state, unfortunately, I find that these are not produced consistently and it is only after warm summers that they may be relied upon. At other times, the plant must be treated as an annual and renewed each year, or possibly a few stock plants overwintered in tanks in a warm greenhouse.
SPREAD Will cover about 1sq m (3sq ft) after one year.

Utricularia vulgaris Bladderwort

> *Even by water garden standards, this is an odd thing, a submerged, floating rootless plant that looks like a mass of green threads covered with tiny pimples. It rises to the surface in summer to thrust flowers that look like tiny orange snapdragons up out of the water. It then sinks again and continues its carnivorous habit, trapping minute aquatic creatures and consuming them. It survives the winter, when light and food are scarce, as dormant buds.*

Utricularia vulgaris

FLOWERS In summer, small, gold-orange, rising above the water's surface and looking like small snapdragons (*Antirrhinum*).
FOLIAGE Deciduous, dark green, tangled hair-like mass of submerged, floating leaves.
SITE Full sun to light shade.
RECOMMENDED POOL SIZE Small to large.
SPECIAL REQUIREMENTS Always best in almost still, slightly acidic water.
HARDINESS Very hardy, tolerating -20°C (-4°F) as dormant buds.
SPREAD Will cover about 50sq cm (20sq in) after about one year.

PLANTING
As young plants in spring, dropped into the water.

CARE
Thin out plants occasionally to limit the spread.

PROPAGATION
By division in spring.

PROBLEMS
None.

RECOMMENDED VARIETIES
A large number of superficially very similar species is available, especially from specialist suppliers. However, you must be sure that any plants that you buy are described as hardy, as some are for aquarium use only. *Utricularia vulgaris* is the commonest and most reliable.

87

CREATING A BOG GARDEN

A bog garden bordering a pool is one of the most delightful ways in which the transition from the pool to the wider garden can be achieved. Such an area makes it possible to grow plants that thrive in constantly-moist ground but that, unlike true aquatics and marginals, will not grow if their roots are in completely waterlogged ground or water.

MOISTURE-LOVING PLANTS

The variety of plants that can be grown in a bog garden is extensive, ranging right through from tall herbaceous plants to low-growing ground cover species. Some bear racemes of tiny flowers while others have interesting foliage to offer instead. These moisture-loving plants often rely on short growing seasons, so they tend to have fast-maturing and vigorous habits. Some of the best known and most reliable bog garden plants are listed on the following pages (see pp.90–1), and they represent the widest possible range, from the spreading and lush, to the upright and dainty. Many well-known and favoured garden plants, including astilbes and *Lysimachia* (loosestrife), thrive in moist, shady ground, but a bog garden will allow you to extend the range of plants you grow to include more unusual forms, such as the eye-catching *Lysichiton* (skunk cabbage), and the lovely *Trollius* (globeflower).

CONSTRUCTION

A bog garden requires an area of permanently moist soil, and many of you may already have just such an area in your garden that could be turned into a bog garden. Poorly drained, rather clayey soil is best, as are areas where the water table is naturally very near the surface.

If no part of your garden is naturally suitable, a bog garden may be constructed easily in a similar way to a pool created with a flexible liner (see pp.26–9). If you are building a pool with a liner, you could take the opportunity to extend the area to one side of the pool to include a bog garden. Where possible, choose a position that is sheltered from drying winds and that is not exposed to the equally drying effects of direct sun. A site in partial or dappled shade is ideal. Excavate the soil to a depth of about 45cm (18in), moving the top soil carefully to one side to re-use if you wish. The liner should be bedded on sand, as for a pool, but it should have several holes punched in it because although a bog garden is permanently damp it should have adequate drainage. Punch the holes at the rate of one hole, about 1cm (½in) in diameter, every square metre (square yard). An area with no means of drainage will quickly become waterlogged, and anaerobic decomposition will take place, leading to foul conditions.

Fill the bog garden with good garden soil (re-use the top soil here if you wish), ideally mixed with well-rotted garden compost and coarse grit in the ratio (by volume) of 3:2:1. It is a good idea to mound the soil in the centre to create a gradient of moisture content in the soil, which permits the growing of a wider range of bog garden plants.

MAINTENANCE

It is very important that the bog garden is not allowed to dry out in summer, and siting it in a naturally low point in the garden will help to guarantee this. Another way to help maintain the moisture content of a bog garden is to channel water from the rainwater drainpipe of a greenhouse or outbuilding to the bog garden through a plastic pipe below the soil's surface. If the bog garden is built next to a pool, make a series of holes no more than 1cm (½in) wide in the wall between them to allow moisture to seep from the pond into the bog area in dry weather, and also to allow excess water to drain from the bog area into the pond during very wet weather.

Bog gardens require regular maintenance, more so, perhaps, than aquatic plants. For this reason, be careful not make a new bog garden so wide that you cannot easily get to all parts of it. New bog gardens should be planted in mid- to late spring. This is also the time when existing clumps of plants that are becoming overgrown and crowded should be lifted and divided. Weeding should be carried out by hand to prevent the liner from being punctured accidentally by your garden fork. Weeds will thrive in the rich, moist soil of the bog garden, so regular weeding throughout the growing season is especially important. In autumn and early winter you may need to protect the crowns of plants that are not reliably hardy.

Candelabra primulas add colour to bog gardens

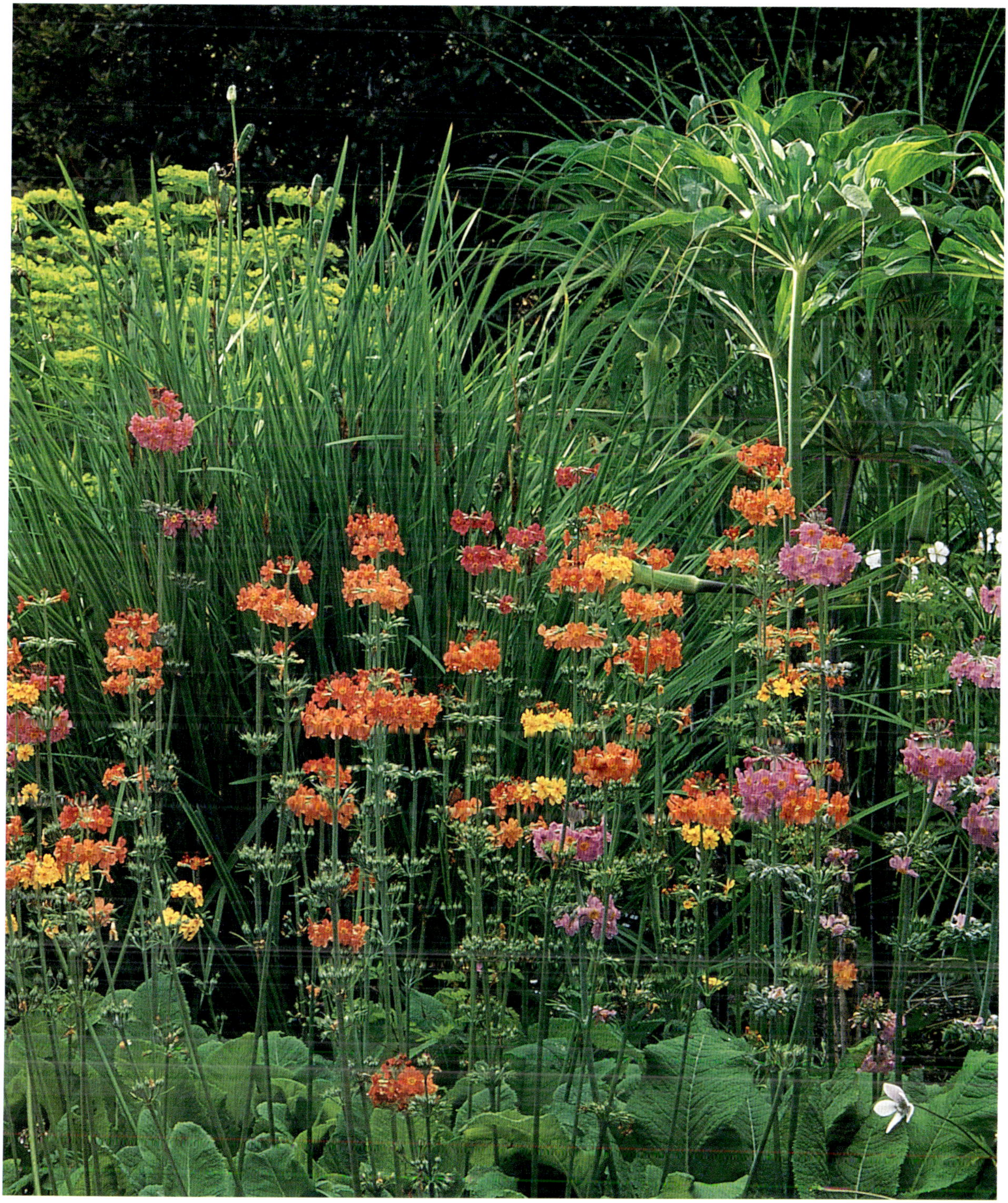

BOG GARDEN PLANTS

The following plants are suitable for a bog garden. The height and spread indicated are those that are likely to be achieved after three years in optimum conditions.

Ajuga reptans **Bugle**
A hardy plant for moderate to deep shade. There are many attractive cultivars with variegated foliage and flowers ranging from purple to light blue. 15 x 90cm (6 x 36in).

Alchemilla mollis **Lady's mantle**
This hardy herbaceous plant prefers dappled shade. The airy, lime green flowers are borne above the pretty leaves. 50 x 50cm (20 x 20in).

Artemisia lactiflora **White mugwort**
A hardy herbaceous plant that bears panicles of tiny flowers above the deeply cut foliage. 1.5 x 0.60m (5 x 2ft).

Arum italicum subsp. *italicum* 'Marmoratum'
The leaves are attractively veined with cream or pale green. The pale spathes are followed by spikes of bright berries. 25 x 15cm (10 x 6in).

Aruncus dioicus **Goat's beard**
A tall hardy herbaceous plant, producing panicles of tiny, whitish flowers. 2 x 1m (6 x 3ft).

Astilbe
Choose a white cultivar of this hardy plant, such as *A.* x *arendsii* 'Irrlicht', 50 x 50cm (20 x 20in), or *A.* 'Professor van der Wielen', 1.2 x 1m (4 x 3ft). Plant in sun.

Bergenia **Elephant's ears**
Good ground cover plants, cultivars with reddish leaves are the most attractive; shade tolerant. 45 x 45cm (18 x 18in).

Brunnera macrophylla
Bright blue flowers are borne in panicles above the heart-shaped leaves. Plant in light to deep shade. 40 x 60cm (16 x 24in).

Campanula lactiflora **Milky bellflower**
This hardy perennial will need staking. Plant in light to moderate shade. 1m x 60cm (3 x 2ft).

Cimicifuga racemosa **Black snake root**
A hardy plant with white flower racemes, unfortunately unpleasantly scented. 1.2m x 60cm (4 x 2ft).

Darmera peltata (syn. *Peltiphyllum peltatum*) **Umbrella plant**
The large leaves appear after the upright stems of white to pink flowers. 1m x 60cm (3 x 2ft).

Iris sibirica 'Pirate Prince'

Dicentra spectabilis 'Alba' **Bleeding heart**
Both the white form of the popular herbaceous plant and *D. formosa alba* will grow in moist, shady ground. Both to about 60 x 45cm (24 x 18in).

Dodecatheon **Shooting stars**
There are several hardy perennials suitable for moist ground in partial shade in this genus. *D. dentatum* has white flowers; 20 x 20cm (8 x 8in). *D. meadia* has rich purple flowers; 40 x 25cm (16 x 10in).

Eupatorium cannabinum **Hemp agrimony**
Pink, purple or white flowers are borne in panicles and will attract butterflies and bees. 1.5m x 60cm (5 x 2ft).

Euphorbia palustris
A hardy, clump-forming perennial for full sun or shade. The flowerheads are bright yellow. 1 x 1m (3 x 3ft).

Filipendula ulmaria **Meadowsweet**
A clump-forming perennial with dense heads of creamy white flowers and dark green leaves. 2 x 1m (6 x 3ft).

Fritillaria meleagris **Snake's head fritillary**
A bulb producing nodding bells of purple, white and chequer patterns. 30 x 15cm (12 x 6in).

Geranium phaeum **Dusky cranesbill**
A clump-forming herbaceous perennial producing deep purple flowers. 60 x 60cm (2 x 2ft).

Geum rivale **Water avens**
An upright perennial with purplish-pink bells. 30 x 20cm (12 x 10in).

Gunnera manicata
A very large perennial, unsuitable for any but a large garden. 2 x 1.5m (6 x 5ft).

Heloniopsis orientalis
Nodding heads of mauve-pink flowers are borne on upright stems above a rosette of evergreen leaves. 30 x 15cm (12 x 6in).

Hosta **Plantain lily**
There is a very wide range of hostas, with leaves in shades of blue and green and different variegations. They have spikes of, usually, blue or mauve flowers. All are irresistible to slugs and snails. 30–90 x 30–60cm (1–3 x 1–2ft).

Iris
Several irises are good choices for a bog garden, notably *Iris innominata*, 25cm (10in) tall, *I. sibirica*, to 1.2m (4ft) tall, *I. orientalis*, to 1m (3ft) tall, and *I. chrysographes*, to 50cm (20in) tall.

Leucojum **Snowflake**
A group of hardy bulbs. *L. aestivum* (summer snowflake) bears little white bells in late spring; 45 x 7.5cm (18 x 3in); *L. vernum* (spring snowflake) bears little white bells in early spring; 30 x 7.5cm (12 x 3in).

Lychnis chalcedonica **Jerusalem cross**
An upright perennial with clusters of scarlet flowers. Grow it in full sun to light shade. 1m x 40cm (36 x 16in).

Lysichiton **Skunk cabbage**
There are two marginal aquatic plants in this genus. *L. americanus*, which has bright yellow spathes; 1 x 1.2m (3 x 4ft), and *L. camtschatcensis*, which has white spathes; 75 x 75cm (30 x 30in).

Lysimachia **Loosestrife**
L. punctata, an upright perennial, has spikes of yellow flowers; 1m x 60cm (3 x 2ft). *L. nummularia* (creeping Jenny) is a prostrate plant, best seen in the golden-leaved form 'Aurea', which grows to 5cm (2in) high and spreads indefinitely.

Lythrum salicaria **Purple loosestrife**
Tall, slender spikes of tiny purple flowers appear from summer to autumn. 1m x 45cm (36 x 18in).

Parochetus communis
A deciduous, spreading plant with pretty, blue, pea-like flowers. 5 x 25cm (2 x 10in).

Persicaria **Bistort**
P. amplexicaulis is a clump-forming, semi-evergreen perennial, producing spikes of pink flowers. Look out for 'Superba', which has dense, pale pink flowers. *P. campanulata*, also a clump-forming, semi-evergreen perennial, bears panicles of fragrant pink or white flowers. Both to 90 x 90cm (3 x 3ft).

Physostegia virginiana **Obedient plant**
A spreading perennial with spikes of flowers in late summer. 'Summer Snow' has white flowers, 60 x 60cm (2 x 2ft). 'Vivid' has purplish-pink flowers; 60 x 30cm (2 x 1ft).

Potentilla palustris **Marsh cinquefoil**
A rhizomatous perennial with dark red to purple flowers in early summer. 45 x 45cm (18 x 18in).

Primula
Several primulas will grow happily in the bog garden, including *P. alpicola*, which has bell-shaped yellow, purple or white flowers; 50 x 30cm (25 x 12in). *P. denticulata* (drumstick primula) has spherical umbels of purple flowers; 45 x 45 (18 x 18in). *P. florindae* (giant cowslip) produces shaggy, yellow flowerheads in early summer; 1.2 x 1m (4 x 3ft).

Pulmonaria **Lungwort**
These low-growing perennials have spotted leaves and flowers in a range of colours, of which the blue forms are most attractive. 25 x 45cm (10 x 18in).

Rheum palmatum **Chinese rhubarb**
Allow this huge perennial plenty of room. The colours of the foliage and flowers vary according to variety. 2.4 x 1.8m (8 x 6ft).

Rodgersia
These vigorous perennials are not for a dainty garden. *R. aesulifolia* has horse chestnut-like leaves; 1.5m x 60cm (5 x 2ft). *R. pinnata* has deeply divided leaves and white flowers; 1.2m x 75cm (4 x 2½ft).

Saururus cernuus **Swamp lily**
The little, fragrant, cream-coloured flowers are borne above the heart-shaped leaves. This plant is an oddity. 30 x 30cm (12 x 12in).

Saxifraga fortunei
A deciduous or semi-evergreen, clump-forming perennial, bearing loose panicles of white flowers. 35 x 30cm (14 x 12in).

Stylophorum diphyllum **Wood poppy**
A perennial forming rosettes of dark green leaves above which the golden-yellow flowers appear. 45 x 45cm (18 x 18in).

Thalictrum flavum **Yellow meadow rue**
A rhizomatous, clump-forming perennial. The little yellow flowers are borne in upright panicles. 1m x 45cm (36 x 18in).

Tiarella cordifolia **Foam flowers**
This can be invasive in rich, moist soil. The little white flowers are borne in upright racemes. 30 x 30cm (12 x 12in).

Tricyrtis hirta **Toad lily**
Purple-spotted white flowers are borne in summer and autumn. 80 x 60cm (32 x 24in).

Trollius europaeus **Common European globeflower**
The spherical golden-yellow flowers, to 5cm (2in) across, are born above the divided leaves. There are several forms of *T. x cultorum* with flowers in shades of yellows, orange and yellowish-red. 80 x 45cm (32 x 18in).

Uvularia grandiflora **Large merry bells**
The yellowish-green, bell-shaped flowers, to 5cm (2in) long, are borne in spring. 75 x 30cm (30 x 12in).

Veratrum nigrum
The reddish-brown flowers, which have an unpleasant scent, are borne in upright spikes. 1.2m x 60cm (4 x 2ft).

CALENDAR OF WATER GARDEN JOBS

EARLY SPRING
- Construct a new pre-formed pool, choosing an open, sunny site
- Prepare the site for a pool made with a butyl liner
- As the fish in an established pool become active, begin to feed them

MID-SPRING
- Plant water lilies and deep-water aquatics, top-dressing pots with shingle or gravel
- Plant underwater oxygenators and marginal aquatics
- Remove any waterplants that were killed by cold weather
- Introduce fish into the pool two weeks after planting
- Tidy established bog gardens, removing large weeds by hand and hoeing carefully around established plants
- Divide perennials in the bog garden
- Plant up a new bog garden
- Plant roots of *Calla palustris* (bog arum) and *Menyanthes trifoliata* (bogbean) near pool margins
- Remove the water heater if you have one and check it before storing it during the summer

LATE SPRING
- Lift water lilies, especially if they have been in place for four years or more
- Check all plants for overcrowding, lifting and dividing as necessary
- Clean old or dirty pools and carry out any repairs that may be needed
- Reinstall pumps and filters, which have been in storage during the winter
- If necessary, use a proprietary algicide to control algae
- Remove algae from surrounding paving and paths

EARLY SUMMER
- Finish planting bog garden plants and aquatic plants
- Throughout summer replace water that is lost through evaporation
- Water the bog garden if necessary
- Keep an eye out for aphids on water lily leaves and the foliage of marginal plants and use a hosepipe to wash them into the water for fish to eat

Planting should wait until the water is fairly warm in spring

MIDSUMMER
- In very hot or thundery weather keep the water aerated by turning on the fountain or waterfall or playing a hosepipe over the surface
- Add more oxygenating plants if the water becomes discoloured
- Control the growth of algae and remove blanket weed

LATE SUMMER
- Continue routine checks on health of fish and plants
- Remove water lily leaves and flowers as they begin to go over
- Deadhead flowers, especially self-seeders, in the bog garden and remove all foliage and flowers
- Save seed of plants such as primulas and sow in the greenhouse
- Cut back excessive growth of submerged oxygenating plants

EARLY AUTUMN
- Remove any dead leaves and be prepared to do this regularly throughout autumn; alternatively, cover the pool's surface with netting to catch the leaves
- Feed the fish so that they can build up reserves before the cold weather begins

MID-AUTUMN
- Begin to excavate the site for a new pond
- Cut down and remove all dead vegetation in and around the pool
- Cut down gunneras and protect the crowns by covering them with the leaves you have cut off
- Lift any plants that are doubtfully hardy and overwinter them in a frost-free place
- Plant new bog garden plants, including bulbs

LATE AUTUMN
- Stop feeding the fish altogether
- If you have a waterfall, fountain or mechanical filter, take out the pump and overhaul it

EARLY WINTER
- Keep the pool topped up with water throughout the winter
- Use straw to protect the crowns of precious plants you have not lifted

MIDWINTER
- Float a rubber ball or piece of expanded polysterene in the pool if you do not have an electric heater
- If ice covers the pool, gently pour in hot water in a corner or stand a pan filled with hot water on the ice to make a hole

LATE WINTER
- If the pool becomes covered with ice, clear away snow so that light can penetrate into the water
- Take advantage of frost-free weather to carry out any repairs

Placing a pool beneath trees will result in leaves to be cleared in autumn

INDEX

Page numbers in *italic* refer to illustrations

Acorus calamus 44, *44*
  'Variegatus' 44
A. gramineus 44
  'Variegatus' 44
Ajuga reptans 90
Alchemilla mollis 90
algae 6, 43
Alhambra 10
Alisma lanceolatum 45
A. plantago-aquatica 44–5, *45*
  var. *parviflorum* 45
Amphibious bistort see *Persicaria amphibia*
animal life 7, 42
aphids 43
Aponogeton distachyos 60, *60*
Arrow arum see *Peltandra undulata*
Arrowhead see *Sagittaria sagittifolia*
Artemisia lactiflora 90
Arum italicum subsp. *italicum* 'Marmoratum' 90
Aruncus dioicus 90
Astilbe 90
A. x arendsii 'Irrlicht' 90
A. 'Professor van der Wielen' 90
autumn 93
Azolla caroliniana 82, *82*
A. filiculoides 82

bentomat 32
bentonite 32
Bergenia 90
Bistort see *Persicaria*
Black snake root see *Cimicifuga racemosa*
Bladderwort see *Utricularia vulgaris*
blanket weed 43
Bleeding heart see *Dicentra spectabilis* 'Alba'
Bog arum see *Calla palustris*
Bog bean see *Menyanthes trifoliata*
bog gardens 39, 88–9
  plants 90–91
Brass buttons see *Cotula coronopifolia*

Brooklime see *Veronica beccabunga*
Brown, Lancelot (Capability) 10
Brunnera macrophylla 90
bubble fountains 16
Bugle see *Ajuga reptans*
building
  bog gardens 88
  water gardens 24–33
Burr reed see *Sparganium erectum*
Butomus umbellatus 45, *45*
butyl liners 27, 35

calculations, flexible liners 27
calendar, jobs 92–3
Calla palustris 46, *46*
Callitriche 74
C. palustris 74
Caltha leptostyla 47
C. palustris 46–7, *47*
  var. 'Alba' 46
  'Flore Pleno' 46
Campanula lactiflora 90
Canadian pondweed see *Elodea canadensis*
Candelabra primula *89*
Cape pondweed see *Aponogeton distachyos*
carp 42
Ceratophyllum demersum 74–5, *75*
Chatsworth 10
children 9, 16
Chinese rhubarb see *Rheum palmatum*
Cimicifuga racemosa 90
clay 32
clay-lined pools 32–3
cleaning pools 34
Common duckweed see *Lemna minor*
Common European globeflower see *Trollius europaeus*
concrete 30–31
concrete-lined pools 30–31
Cotula coronopifolia 47, *47*
  'Cream Buttons' 47
Crassula helmsii 75, *75*
Creeping Jenny see *Lysimachia nummularia*
Curled pondweed see *Potamogeton crispus*

cuttings 41

Darmera peltata 90
Deanery, Berkshire 15
dew pools 32
Dicentra formosa alba 90
D. spectabilis 'Alba' 90
diseases 43
division 41
Dodecatheon 90
D. dentatum 90
D. meadia 90
Drumstick primula see *Primula denticulata*
Duckweed see *Lemna*
Dusky cranesbill see *Geranium phaeum*

edging 25
Eichhornia crassipes 82–3, *83*
electricity 22
Eleocharis acicularis 76, *76*
Elephant's ears see *Bergenia*
Elodea callitrichoides 76
E. canadensis 6, 7, 76–7, *76*
E. crispa 76
E. densa 76
E. nuttallii 76
emptying pools 34
Equisetum hyemale 48, *48*
Eupatorium cannabinum 90
Euphorbia palustris 90
excavation 25, 27

Fairy moss see *Azolla caroliniana*
feeding 40
Filipendula ulmaria 90
filters 43
fish 7, 36–7, 42
flexible liners 12, 26–9, 35
Flitcroft, Henry 20
Floating heart see *Nymphoides peltata*
floating plants 38, 82–7
Flowering rush see *Butomus umbellatus*
Foam flowers see *Tiarella cordifolia*
Fontinalis antipyretica 77, *77*
formal pools 10–11, 21, 29
fountains 16, 22–3
Fringed water lily see *Nymphoides peltata*
Fritillaria meleagris 90

Frogbit see *Hydrocharis morsus-ranae*
frogs 42
functions, water gardens 6–7
fungal leaf spots 43

Geranium phaeum 90
Geum rivale 90
Giant cowslip see *Primula florindae*
Globeflower see *Trollius*
Goat's beard see *Aruncus dioicus*
Golden club see *Orontium aquaticum*
golden orfe 42
golden rudd 42
goldfish 42
Great purple monkey flower see *Mimulus lewisii*
Great reedmace see *Typha latifolia*
green slime 43
Gunnera manicata 90

half-barrels 18
Heloniopsis orientalis 90
Hemp agrimony see *Eupatorium cannabinum*
Hestercombe, Somerset 15
Hidcote Manor, Gloucestershire 11
Hippuris vulgaris 60–61, *61*
Hoare II, Henry 20
Hornwort see *Ceratophyllum demersum*
Hosta 91
Hottonia palustris 83, *83*
Houttuynia cordata 48–9, *49*
Hydrocharis morsus-ranae 6, 84, *84*
Hypericum elodes 49, *49*
hypertufa 18–19

ice 37
informal pools 12
Iris 91
I. chrysographes 91
I. ensata 50, *50*
  'Alba' 50

Higo hybrids 50
  'Moonlight Waves' 50
  'Rose Queen' 50
  'Variegata' 50
I. innominata 91
I. laevigata 50
  'Alba' 50
  'Atropurpurea' 50
  'Colchesterensis' 50
  'Variegata' 50, *51*
  'Weymouth Midnight' 50
I. orientalis 91
I. pseudacorus 50, *51*
  'Alba' 50
  var. *bastardii* 50
  'Variegata' 50
I. sibirica 91
  'Pirate Prince' 90
I. versicolor 50
  'Kermesina' 50
Ivy-leaved duckweed see *Lemna trisulca*

Japanese influences 20
Jerusalem cross see *Lychnis chalcedonica*

koi 42

Lady's mantle see *Alchemilla mollis*
lakes 20
Large merry bells see *Uvularia grandiflora*
Latour-Marliac, Joseph Bory 69
Lavender musk see *Mimulus ringens*
leaks, repairing 31, 35–7
Lemna 85
L. gibba 85, *85*
L. minor 85
L. polyrhiza 85
L. trisulca 85
Lesser reedmace see *Typha angustifolia*
Leucojum 91
L. aestivum 91
L. vernum 91
light 8
lighting 23
liners
  flexible 12, 26–9, 35
  pre-formed 24–5, 36
Lobelia cardinalis 51
L. dortmanna 51, 78, *78*

94

L. fulgens 51
L. 'Queen Victoria' 51, *51*
Loosestrife see *Lysimachia*
Lungwort see *Pulmonaria*
Lutyens, Edward 15
Lychnis chalcedonica 91
Lysichiton 88, 91
L. americanus 91
L. camtschatcensis 91
Lysimachia 88, 91
L. nummularia 91
  'Aurea' 91
L. punctata 91
Lythrum salicaria 91

maintenance
  bog gardens 88
  water gardens 34–7
Mare's tail see *Hippuris vulgaris*
marginal zone 12
marginals 38–9, 44–59
Marsh cinquefoil see *Potentilla palustris*
Marsh St John's wort see *Hypericum elodes*
Meadowsweet see *Filipendula ulmaria*
Mentha aquatica 52, *52*
Menyanthes trifoliata 52–3
mildew 43
Milky bellflower see *Campanula lactiflora*
Mimulus 53
M. × *hartonianus* 53
M. lewisii 53
M. luteus 53, *53*
M. moschatus 53
M. ringens 53
minnows 42
moisture-loving plants 88
Monkey musk see *Mimulus moschatus*
Musk see *Mimulus*
Myosotis scorpioides 54, *54*
  'Mermaid' 54
  'Pinkie' 54
Myriophyllum 78–9
M. aquaticum 78, *79*, 79
M. spicatum 6, 78, 79
M. verticillatum 78, 79, 79

newts 42
Nuphar 62
N. japonica 62, *62*
N. lutea 62, *62*
N. pumila 62

N. variegata 62
Nymphaea 64–9
N. alba 20–21, 65, 67
N. 'Albatross' 68
N. 'Amabilis' 65, 67
N. 'Atropurpurea' 67
N. 'Attraction' 67
N. 'Aurora' 68
N. 'Brackleyi Rosea' 68
N. 'Caroliniana Nivea' 67
N. 'Charles de Meurville' 67
N. 'Colonel A.J. Welch' 67
N. 'Colossea' 65, 67
N. 'Commanche' 68
N. 'Conqueror' 67
N. 'Ellisiana' 68
N. 'Escarboucle' 67
N. 'Fabiola' 65
N. 'Firecrest' 68
N. 'Froebelii' 68, *68*
N. 'Gladstoneana' 20–21, 67
N. 'Gloire du Temple-sur-Lot' 67
N. 'Gloriosa' 68
N. 'Gonnäre' 65, 67
N. 'Graziella' 68
N. × *helvola* 68, *68*
N. 'Indiana' 68
N. 'James Brydon' 19, 68, *68*
N. 'Laydekeri Fulgens' 68
N. 'Laydekeri Lilacea' 68
N. 'Laydekeri Purpurata' 68
N. 'Madame Wilfron Gonnäre' 64, 67
N. 'Marliacea Albida' 67
N. 'Marliacea Carnea' 67
N. 'Marliacea Chromatella' 65, 67
N. 'Marliacea Rosea' 65, 67
N. 'Masaniello' 65, 67
N. 'Moorei' 65, 67, 69
N. 'Mrs Richmond' 67
N. odorata 67
N. 'Odorata Sulphurea Grandiflora' 68
N. 'Odorata William B. Shaw' 67
N. 'Paul Hariot' 68
N. 'Pygmaea Helvola' 19
N. 'Pygmaea Rubra' 19
N. 'René Gérard' 66, 67
N. 'Robinsoniana' 68

N. 'Rose Arey' 68
N. 'Sioux' 68
N. 'Solfatare' 68
N. 'Sunrise' 67
N. tetragona 19, 68
N. tuberosa
  'Richardsonii' 67
  'Rosea' 67
N. 'William Falconer' 67
Nymphoides peltata 63, *63*
  'Bennettii' 63

Obedient plant see *Physostegia virginiana*
Orontium aquaticum 70, *70*
oxygenators 6–7

Parochetus communis 91
Peltandra undulata 54–5, 55
Persicaria 91
P. amphibia 71, *71*
P. amplexicaulis 91
  'Superba' 91
P. campanulata 91
pests 43
Physostegia virginiana 91
  'Summer Show' 91
  'Vivid' 91
Pickerel weed see *Pontederia cordata*
planting 12, 14, 30
Plantain lily see *Hosta*
planting 6–7, 40
  tub gardens 19
planting baskets 40
plants
  bog gardens 90–91
  care 36
  floating 38, 82–7
  moisture-loving 88
  submerged 38, 74–81
  type 38–9
  water 38, 60 73
polyethylene sheeting 26–7
polyvinyl chloride (PVC) 27
Pond lily see *Nuphar*
Pondweed see *Potamogeton*
Pontederia alba 72
P. azurea 72
P. cordata 72, *72*
P. lancifolia 72
pools
  clay-lined 32–3

concrete-lined 30–31
formal 10–11, 21, 29
informal 12
large still-water 20–21
maintenance 34–7
pre-formed 12, 24–5, 36
raised 11, 24, 29
size 4, 6, 12
sunken 11, 24–5
position, informal pools 12
Potamogeton 80
P. crispus 6, 80
P. pectinatus 80, *80*
Potentilla palustris 91
pre-formed pools 12, 24–5, 36
Primula 91
P. alpicola 91
P. denticulata 91
P. florindae 91
propagation 41
puddled clay 32
Pulmonaria 91
Purple loosestrife see *Lythrum salicaria*

raised pools 11, 24, 29
Ranunculus 55
R. aquatilis 81, *81*
R. flammula 55
R. lingua 55, *55*
  'Grandiflorus' 55
Reedmace see *Typha*
reflections 8
repairing leaks 31, 35–7
Rheum palmatum 91
rills 15
Rodgersia 91
R. aesulifolia 91
R. pinnata 91
running water 14

safety 9, 23
Sagittaria sagittifolia 56, *56*
  'Flore Pleno' 56
Saururus cernuus 91
Saxifraga fortunei 91
Scouring rush see *Equisetum hyemale*
seed 41
shade 6, 8
shape, formal pools 10–11
Shooting stars see *Dodecatheon*
shubunkins 42
shuttering 30
sinks 18–19

sites, water gardens 8–9
size, pools 4, 6, 12
Skunk cabbage see *Lysichiton*
slopes 9
snails 7, 42
Snake's head fritillary see *Fritillaria meleagris*
Snowflake see *Leucojum*
soupy water 43
Sparganium erectum 73, 73
Spearwort see *Ranunculus*
Spike rush see *Eleocharis acicularis*
spouts 16
spring 92
Spring snowflake see *Leucojum vernum*
still-water pools, large 20–21
Stourhead, Wiltshire 20
Stratiotes aloides 86, *86*
streams 14–15
style, formal pools 10–11
Stylophorum diphyllum 91
submerged plants 38, 74–81
summer 92–3
Summer snowflake see *Leucojum aestivum*
sunken pools 11, 24–5
sunlight 8
Swamp lily see *Saururus cernuus*
Sweet flag see *Acorus calamus*

Thalictrum flavum 91
Tiarella cordifolia 91
Tintinhull, Gloucestershire 21
Toad lily see *Tricyrtis hirta*
Trapa natans 6, 86–7, *87*
trees 8
Tricyrtis hirta 91
Trollius 88
T. × *cultorum* 91
T. europaeus 91
tub gardens 18–19
Typha 56–7
T. angustifolia 57, *57*
T. latifolia 57, *57*
T. laxmannii 57
T. minima 56, 57, *57*

Umbrella plant see *Darmera peltata*

95

INDEX

Utricularia vulgaris 87, *87*
Uvularia grandiflora 91

Veratrum nigrum 91
Veronica beccabunga 58, *58*

wall-mounted fountains 16
Water avens see *Geum rivale*
Water chestnut see *Trapa natans*
water clarity 43
Water crowfoot see *Ranunculus aquatilis*
water features 16
Water forget-me-not see *Myosotis scorpioides*

water gardens
 building 24–33
 function 6–7
 maintenance 34–7
 plans 12
 site 8–9
Water hawthorn see *Aponogeton distachyos*
Water hyacinth see *Eichornia crassipes*
Water irises 50
Water lilies 6, 8, 38
 fountains 23
 large still-water pools 20–21
 tub gardens 19

see also *Nuphar*; *Nymphaea*
water lily beetles 43
Water lobelia see *Lobelia dortmanna*
Water milfoil see *Myriophyllum*
Water mint see *Mentha aquatica*
Water moss see *Fontinalis antipyretica*
Water musk see *Mimulus luteus*
Water plantain see *Alisma plantago-aquatica*
water plants 38, 60–73

Water soldier see *Stratiotes aloides*
Water starwort see *Callitriche*
Water violet see *Hottonia palustris*
waterfalls 23
White mugwort see *Artemisia lactiflora*
Willow grass see *Persicaria amphibia*
Willow moss see *Fontinalis antipyretica*
wind 8
wind breaks 8–9
winter 93
Wolffia arrhiza 85

Wood poppy see *Stylophorum diphyllum*

Yellow meadow rue see *Thalictrum flavum*
Yellow musk see *Mimulus luteus*

Zantedeschia aethiopica 58–9
 'Crowborough' 59, *59*
 'Green Goddess' 59, *59*

PHOTOGRAPHIC ACKNOWLEDGEMENTS

Front Jacket: Harpur Garden Library/Jerry Harpur, Great Barr, Birmingham, Design:Ernie Taylor
Back Jacket: Garden Picture Library/Rex Butcher
James Allison 46, 62 Right
Aquila Photographics J Mathieson 24, 25, 26
A-Z Botanical Collection Bjorn Svensson 48
Pat Brindley 57 Left, 61
Bruce Coleman Ltd. Hans Reinhard 87 Top Left
Eric Crichton 4, 39, 45 Right, 51 Top Right, 55 Bottom, 65 Centre, 65 Centre Right
John Fielding 47 Left, 75 Bottom Centre, 79 Top
Garden Picture Library 2–3/David England 79 Bottom/Christi Carter 89/John Glover 9, 19, 37/Michael Howes 92/Jane Legate 36/Marie O'Hara 11/Gary Rogers 30
John Glover 5, 14, 21, 23, 28, 51 Top Left, 70/Farm Fields, Sanderstead, Design: Alan Titchmarsh 18/High Meadow, Surrey 7
Octopus Publishing Group Ltd. 51 Bottom Left
Harpur Garden Library /RSH Chelsea 1994, Merrist Wood 8/Sun House 17/Sun House, Long Melford 31/Weslay & Susan Dixon, Lake Forest 20
Andrew Lawson 2 Insert Top, 29, 33, 45 Left, 54, 64, 65 Bottom Left, 65 Bottom Right, 68 Left, 68 Centre, 69, 82, 90, 93/Designer: Simon Johnson 13
S & O Mathews 15
Natural Image Bob Gibbons 52, 60, 77, 78, 80, 83 Left, 87 Bottom Right
National Trust Photographic Library /Stephen Robson 22
Nature Photographers Ltd. Jean Hall 44, 86, David Rae 47 Right, Paul Sterry 75 Top Right, LG Jessup 56/Roger Tidman 62 Left
Photos Horticultural 1, 10, 38, 43, 58, 59 Top, 59 Bottom, 65 Top Left, 65 Top Right, 66, 68 Right, 75 Top Left, 76 Bottom
Premaphotos Wildlife 84, 85/K G Preston 63
Harry Smith Collection 34, 35, 40, 42, 49, 49 Right, 50, 53, 55 Top, 57 right, 57 Centre, 65 Top Centre, 65 Centre Left, 65 Bottom Centre, 71, 72, 73, 74, 76 Top, 81
Elizabeth Whiting & Associates 83 Right

TEMPERATURE CHART

BARELY HARDY	0 to -5°C	32 to 23°F
FAIRLY HARDY	-5 to -10°C	23 to 14°F
MODERATELY HARDY	-10 to -15°C	14 to 5°F
HARDY	-15 to -20°C	5 to -4°F
VERY HARDY	-20°C or below	-4°F or below